Original publication: "Klíčkův notýsek"
Author: Eva Šašinková, M.M., Ph.D., M.B.A.
Illustrations: Mgr. Kateřina Kovářová
Original graphic design: Lumír Kaděra
Original publisher: Czech Music Edition, Prague, Czech Republic, 2022
Website: www.hudebni-publikace.cz
Copyright: Eva Šašinková, M.M., Ph.D., M.B.A.
Original Czech version ISBN: 978-80-908169-7-8

English adaptation: "Clefi's Little Notebook"
Illustrations: Mgr. Kateřina Kovářová
Translation, adaptation, and graphic design: Roman Placzek, D.M.A.
Publisher: BumbleBeeNotes™ Music Publishing, Manlius, NY, USA, 2024
Catalog number: cbbn002-wb-001
Website: www.bumblebeenotes.com
Copyright: BumbleBee Notes™ Inc. Music Corporation
ISBN: 979-8-9919035-0-9

What I want to know:

Sounds

Clefs

Keyboard

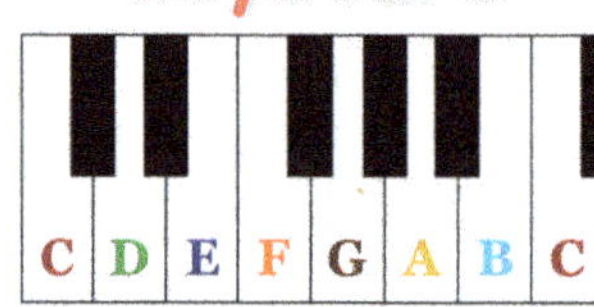

Notes

Music Staff

Rests

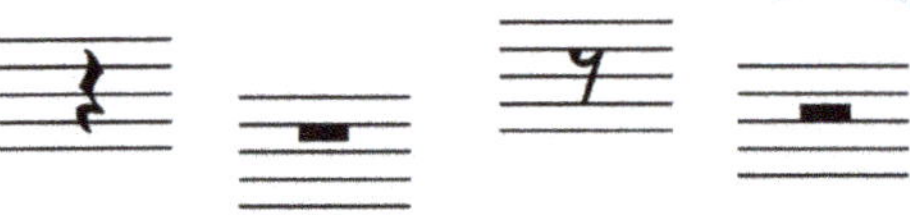

Eva Šašinková, M.M., Ph.D., MBA, the author of the series, lives in Prague, Czech Republic, where she concertizes and holds academic positions at the Pilsen Conservatory and Academy of Music in Prague. Since childhood, Eva has dreamed of becoming a music teacher, sharing her passion for music, especially with children. She has a deep love for the double bass, her instrument, for which she holds a master's degree. However, Eva also profoundly admires the piano, an instrument that was an inseparable part of her childhood.

This admiration is the reason for her method's concept, which is based on the keyboard's layout. Eva is convinced that the piano is a unique instrument designed to help explain the fundamentals of music theory, the meaning of tones and melody, and the mission of music. She successfully proves her firm conviction in the practical application of her method. The story of her project started with a children's story that came to life during a trying period in the author's life.

Her passion for teaching children and desire to share her knowledge helped her concentrate on the essentials. During her pedagogical activities, Eva noticed that the materials available to her for the curriculum presentation were, in her professional opinion, unsatisfactory. She began visiting music schools in her home country, the Czech Republic, comparing, editing, reworking, and creating. As a result, Eva began bringing worksheets filled with information and fun activities to the music education classes to make students' time learning music theory more engaging, accessible, and entertaining. The reactions of the young music students and fellow pedagogues were overwhelmingly positive.

Professor Eva engaged children's senses from every angle—drawing, singing, and keyboard demonstrations—everything children appreciated. On top of that, she had "The Story of a Song, "which kicked off a star career for one little boy, Clefi. He welcomes children in his "Clefi's Little Notebook" and helps them learn more in the four volumes of his "Clefi's Music Notebook." He plays and sings with them in "Clefi's Little Music Education Notebook" (in the translated version integrated into "Clefi's Little Notebook" – editor's note) and "Clefi's Musical Instruments" written for little musicians. Clefi helps them practice their newly acquired knowledge in three workbooks full of fun tasks and exercises. Children play with little Clefi, learn, and get ready for the more dedicated encounter with Lady Music and their chosen instrument in a fun and engaging way. And maybe it will become the love of their lives, their calling, and a hobby, as it happened to the author.

And to the sad faces of those who did not have the luck to learn from the best teachers and publications and did not have the best opportunities, Eva says with her clever little smile: "If you love music and have an open heart, the muse will not ask you how old you are. She will kiss you on the brow when you least expect it. **So do not wait and be ready!**"

AUTHOR'S FOREWORD

Clefi's New Music Education School
is a unified music education method for children,
amateur musicians, and music students.
Based on my extensive multi-genre musical
performing career, many years of experience
teaching children, and my terminal education
degree in music theory, I have created a unified
music education program for children from an
early age to young musicians who choose to
study music more seriously. The New Music
Education School leans on children's natural
perception of music. It offers young musicians
and their teachers a unified educational system
of fundamental music theory, aiming to support
musical creativity. Its main goal is to awaken
children's musicianship, based on creativity and
the ability to sing a song, play it on a musical
instrument of their choice, and write it down
correctly —the sort of musicianship that enables
them to use their musical knowledge
theoretically and practically.
The first book, **Clefi's Little Notebook**, is
tailored for the youngest musicians. It
introduces us to Clefi, a charming little boy who
shares his story. Clefi becomes our companion
on this musical adventure. In Clefi's Little
Notebook, children delve into musical notation,
the birth of a song, a musical note, a musical
staff, a clef (which inspired Clefi's name), the
musical alphabet, and a scale. They learn to
read and write notes in the fourth, the middle
octave, and practice their new skills through
exercises, puzzles, engaging tasks, and songs
they play and sing.
Clefi's Music Notebooks 1, 2, 3, and **4**
follow Clefi's Little Notebook. These four full-
color music textbooks stand out for their unique
conceptual design. Each volume is a complete
unit and can be used individually.
At the same time, all four volumes are designed
as a single method, seamlessly following one
another, so that the children can acquire a
complete understanding of the fundamentals of
music theory in a friendly and engaging way.
Beautiful illustrations and graphic design
enhance the unique quality of these lovely
publications. All textbooks are suitable for
children, amateur musicians, and professional
music students.
This music education series explains the
fundamentals of music theory quickly and
efficiently so that children can understand and
practice them while playing musical instruments,
singing, and harmonizing. The textbooks aim to
develop children's musical abilities, aural skills,
perception of tone pitch and duration, and
rhythmical and tonal melodic structure.
The idea behind this methodological concept is
to make children first listen, then understand,
learn, utilize, and create. When a baby is born, it
listens and absorbs speech. When it understands
it, it tries to pronounce the first words. A child
attempts to understand the connections and
context. Only after several years can a child
logically think and systematically create. And the
same applies to the understanding of music!
What would the knowledge of music theory be
for if we did not listen to music and didn't use the
ingenious system of music theory in practice?
However, the same applies both ways. How can
we expect to evolve in our music-making if we
refuse to learn and explore the mysteries of
music, its tonal relations, harmony, and rhythm?
This method will help children fully absorb
music and learn essential human and life values.
We can learn to read and write only if we listen
to our parents talk from an early age. Then, we
learn the words, pronounce them, and
understand their meaning. The same applies to
music and how we understand it.
I hope my books will bring
you joy and help many young
musicians open the door to
the beautiful world of music.

What's Inside:

Dear Little Music Stars,

Welcome to my music school! I'm so excited to have you here! Learning to sing or play an instrument can seem like a big adventure, but we're going to make it super fun together!

By the time we finish this book, everything will be so easy and enjoyable. You'll see how music can bring us smiles, laughter, and joy!

Let's have a great time making music together!

Hugs,

Clefi

SOUNDS

We have five senses. Can you name them? Which of them do we need to play musical instruments?

 **Hearing**

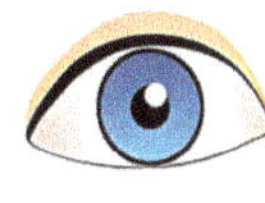 **Sight**

 **Touch**

 **Smell**

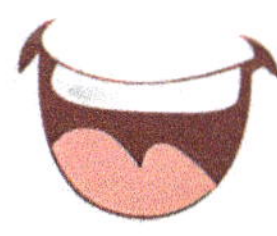 **Taste**

We sense **sounds** by hearing.

- **Ordinary sounds** are swishing, random noises, screeching, thunder, or rain.

- **Musical sounds** are those we can **sing** or **play** using **musical instruments**.

E Draw something that makes an **ordinary** sound.

 MUSICAL SOUNDS. Describe what you see in the picture.
Point at things that make **musical sounds** and try to **imitate** them.
Then, **color** the picture.

MUSICAL SOUND

Musical sounds can be produced using musical instruments.
Musical sounds are divided into **rhythmic** and **melodic**.

- The **rhythmic musical sounds** are played on **rhythm instruments**.

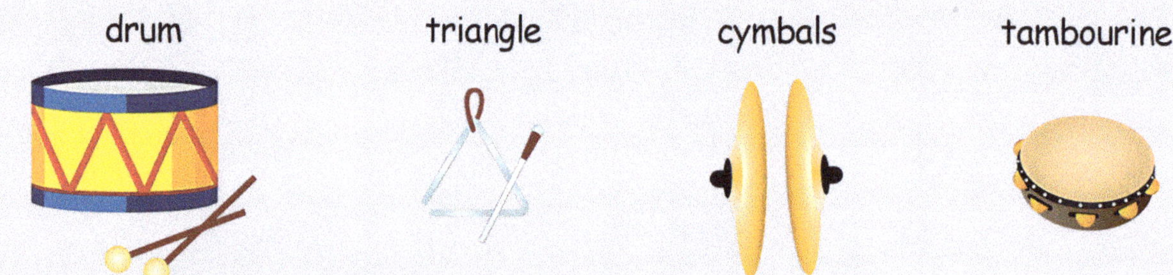

- The **melodic musical sounds** are played on **melodic musical instruments**.

E Draw musical instruments that make **rhythmic musical sounds**.

TONE

A **tone** is a melodic musical sound.

Tones have:
- Volume
- Color
- Pitch
- Duration

 Draw something that makes **tones**.

 Color the balloons with the **ordinary** sounds yellow ●.
Color the balloons with the **tones** red ●, and then, color the boy **Clefi**.

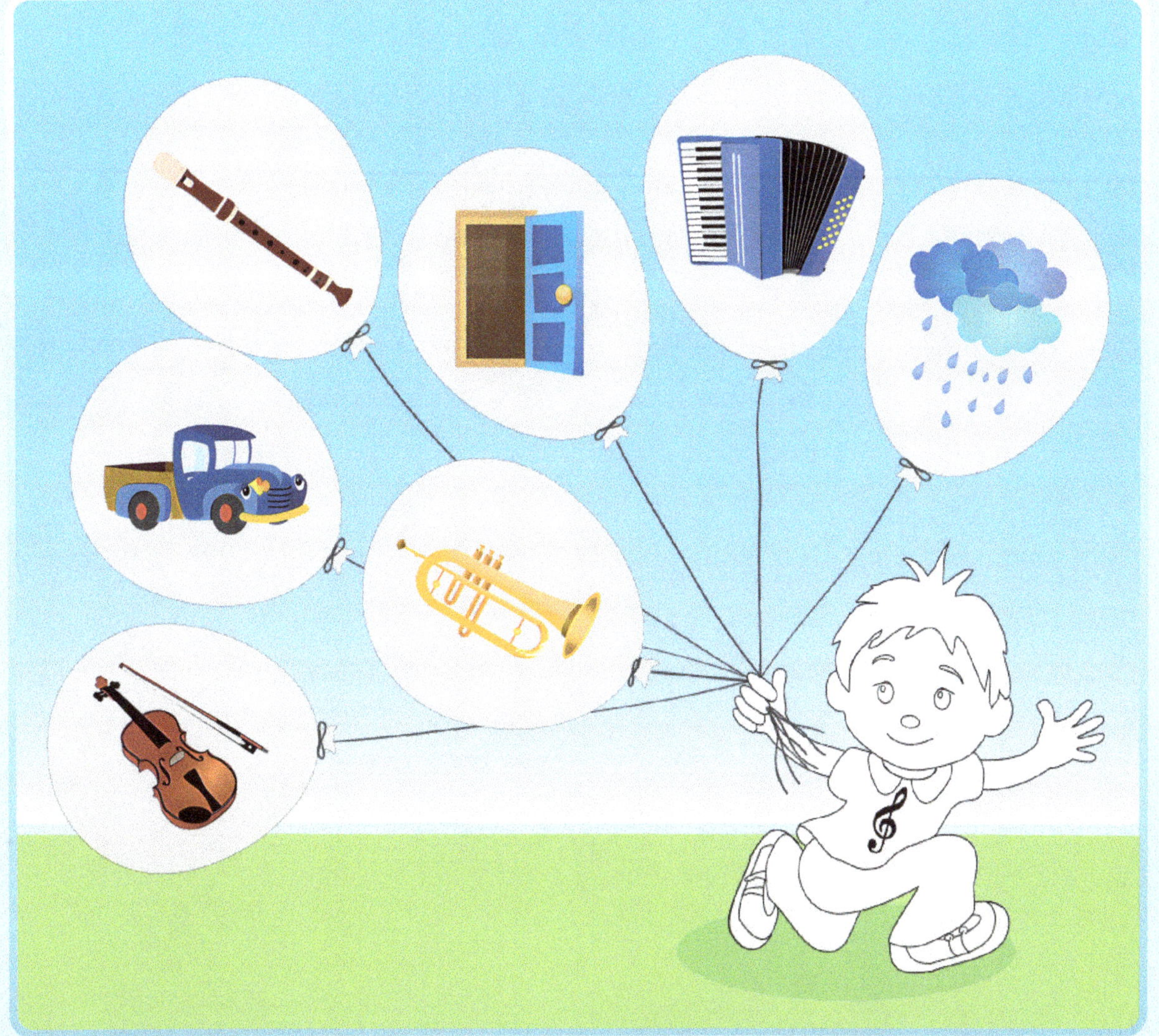

TONE VOLUME

Tones can be **loud** or **soft**.

- **In music, we mark the loud tones with the letter f.**

$$\boldsymbol{f} = \text{forte} = \text{loudly}$$

- **In music, we mark the soft tones with the letter p.**

$$\boldsymbol{p} = \text{piano} = \text{softly}$$

E — Try saying words **loudly** and **softly** and describe them as **forte** or **piano**.
Sing or play any musical instrument **loudly - forte** and **softly - piano**.

E — Color the birds singing "p" - **piano** = softly yellow ●.
Color the birds singing "f" - **forte** = loudly blue ●.

TONE COLOR

Tones also have **colors**. If we play the **same tone** on **different musical instruments**, it will have a **different color**.

When each of us sings the same song, we will recognize who is singing. We all have a **different voice color**.

E | Close your eyes and **guess instruments** according to the **color** of their **tone**.

E | Sing with your friends, and **guess who is singing** by the **color** of their **voice**.

E | Draw one of the **musical instruments** you were listening to.

TONE PITCH

Tones can be **high** and **low**.

- **High tones** are played by a **flute** or a **violin**, for example.

- **Low tones** are played by a **bass** (double bass), for example.

Let's learn to recognize the **pitch of the tones**.
We will mark them with dashes positioned at **different heights**.

E Learn the following songs from the Clefi's Songbook at the end of the book. **Sing** the songs and **show with your hand rising** (ascending) and **falling** (descending) **pitches** of the **tones**.

sheep peep
tle a
Lit- Not

Songbook page 51

On Our
the pear
tree tree

Songbook page 52

Go sleep lit- star-
to tle
my light

Songbook page 52

der a fence but
Boo hid un-

Songbook page 53

E

Sing the songs according to the pictures. Show with your hand the **rising** and **falling melody**. Can you match the correct houses?
Connect the **belonging houses** and color their roofs with the **same color**.

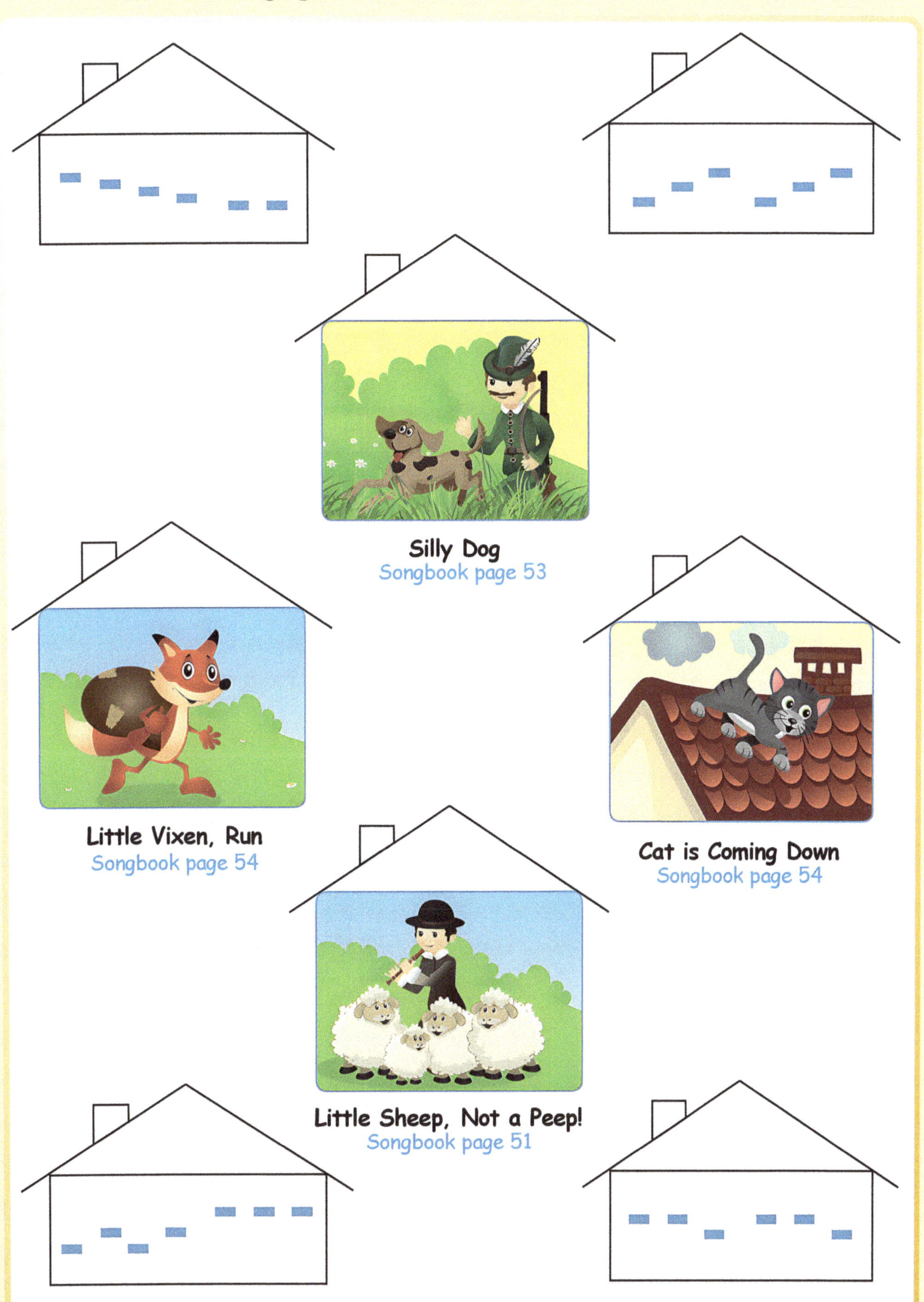

Silly Dog
Songbook page 53

Little Vixen, Run
Songbook page 54

Cat is Coming Down
Songbook page 54

Little Sheep, Not a Peep!
Songbook page 51

TONE LENGTH - DURATION

Tones can be **short** and **long**.

- Let's mark the **short tones** with a **dot**. ●
- Let's mark the **long tones** with a **dash**. ▬

E Let's sing **short** and **long tones** using the **syllables** "*la*" ● and "*laah*" ▬ .

E Can you tell which animal made the **short** and which the **long tone**?

(The teacher sings or plays animal sounds in short and long tones, and children fill in a dot or a dash into the frames below the picture of the animal.)

The songs can have **short** and **long tones**. To see the difference, we mark the **short tones** with **dots** and the **long tones** with **dashes**. It's always good to clap the songs first to hear the tones' **length - duration**. Notice that when clapping the **long tones**, our hands **stay together longer**.

E Learn and **sing** the song *Cat is Coming Down* while **clapping** the length of the tones. Then, **color** the cat. Songbook page 54

• • • •   — — — — — —

Cat is com-ing   down and   meo-wing,   meo-wing

• • • •   — — — — — —

On the roof, the   wind is   how - ling   how - ling

E Learn the three children's folk songs from Clefi's Little Songbook, then **sing** and **clap** them. Connect the **bubbles** with dots and dashes with the **correct songs**.

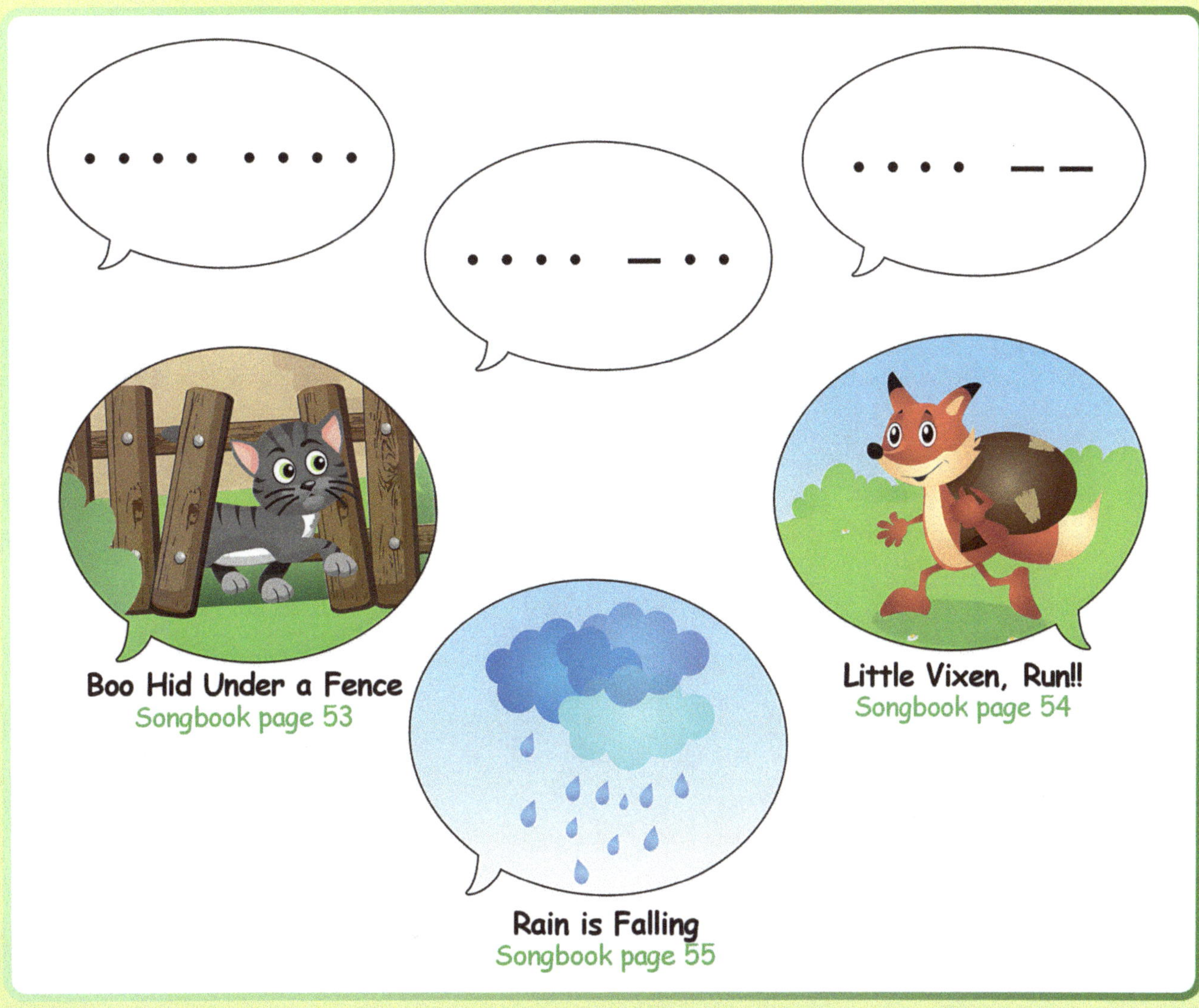

Boo Hid Under a Fence
Songbook page 53

Rain is Falling
Songbook page 55

Little Vixen, Run!!
Songbook page 54

THE STORY OF A SONG

Once upon a time, a little old house stood next to a green forest. In this house lived a kind elderly lady and her loving husband. Though they had no children, they were blessed with a playful dog named Rex and a mischievous cat named Boo, who delighted in chasing each other around. During this time, many people faced hardship and poverty. The couple had only their cozy home with a small garden surrounded by an old picket fence. Behind the fence lay an orchard and a small field where they tended to their crops. However, they often felt a sense of sadness, as the people of their time did not know any songs to lift their spirits—there were no songs to sing **yet**.

One beautiful morning, the Sun rose, gently touching the rooftops with its golden rays. It soon spotted the little house of an elderly couple and decided to bring some joy into their lives. The Sun extended its shimmering rays to their doorstep and laid down a small bundle with a little boy inside. Dressed in a shirt adorned with a musical clef, the boy was a delightful surprise. When the elderly couple first saw him, they were astonished, trying to understand where the boy had come from. However, when they looked up to the sky, they noticed the beam of sunlight reaching to the baby. With warm hearts, the gentle old lady and her loving husband welcomed the boy into their home and named him **Clefi**.

When Clefi was your age, dear children, he found great joy in assisting his grandparents in every possible way. What made Clefi even more intriguing was his love for humming and singing since he was just a baby. Those around him were quite curious about this talent. You see, during that time, people had yet to discover the art of singing or creating songs. They thought Clefi was simply mimicking birds. However, a song is something completely different. A song has melody and words. Unlike birds, people can speak and use words to describe their observations, interests, and feelings—like joy or sorrow—allowing them to combine words with melody. When we sing the words, a simple melody is transformed into a beautiful song. And that's exactly what happened to **Clefi**.

One day, Clefi sat on the steps of the little house, observing the clouds as they attempted to obscure the Sun. He spotted their dog, Rex, by the open window, also staring at the darkening sky. In a flash, the little kitty, Boo, darted under the fence, just as Rex leaped out of the window. Witnessing this, Clefi began to sing: ***"Boo hid under a fence, but Rex could see…"***

After the first song, more songs followed. As people heard them, they joined in singing. When they saw something interesting or nice, something that made them happy or sad, they would make a song about it and sing it. And when somebody sings such a song, and someone else learns it and sings it, very soon, everyone sings it. And so thanks to little boy and his love for music people started to sing and music made their lives richer and **beautiful**.

THE END

When people sing a **song** that originated from ordinary people - **folk** and pass it on through the generations, it becomes a FOLK SONG.

A song has:

- **Tones = melody,** which we sing or play using a musical instrument. Tones are written down using **musical notes**.

- **Letters = lyrics,** which describe the content. Lyrics are written down using **words**.

TONES & LETTERS

The **TONES** are written down using **musical notes**.
Musical notes of different pitches lined up in a row create a **melody**.

The **LETTERS** create **words**.
Words that are organized in rhyming sentences create **lyrics**.

Words are written down with **letters** and tones with **notes**.
Color the **balloons** with notes in red and those with letters in blue.

E Color the picture of singing **Clefi** with his chirping friend **Birdy**.

Learn to draw Clefi's friend **Birdy**.

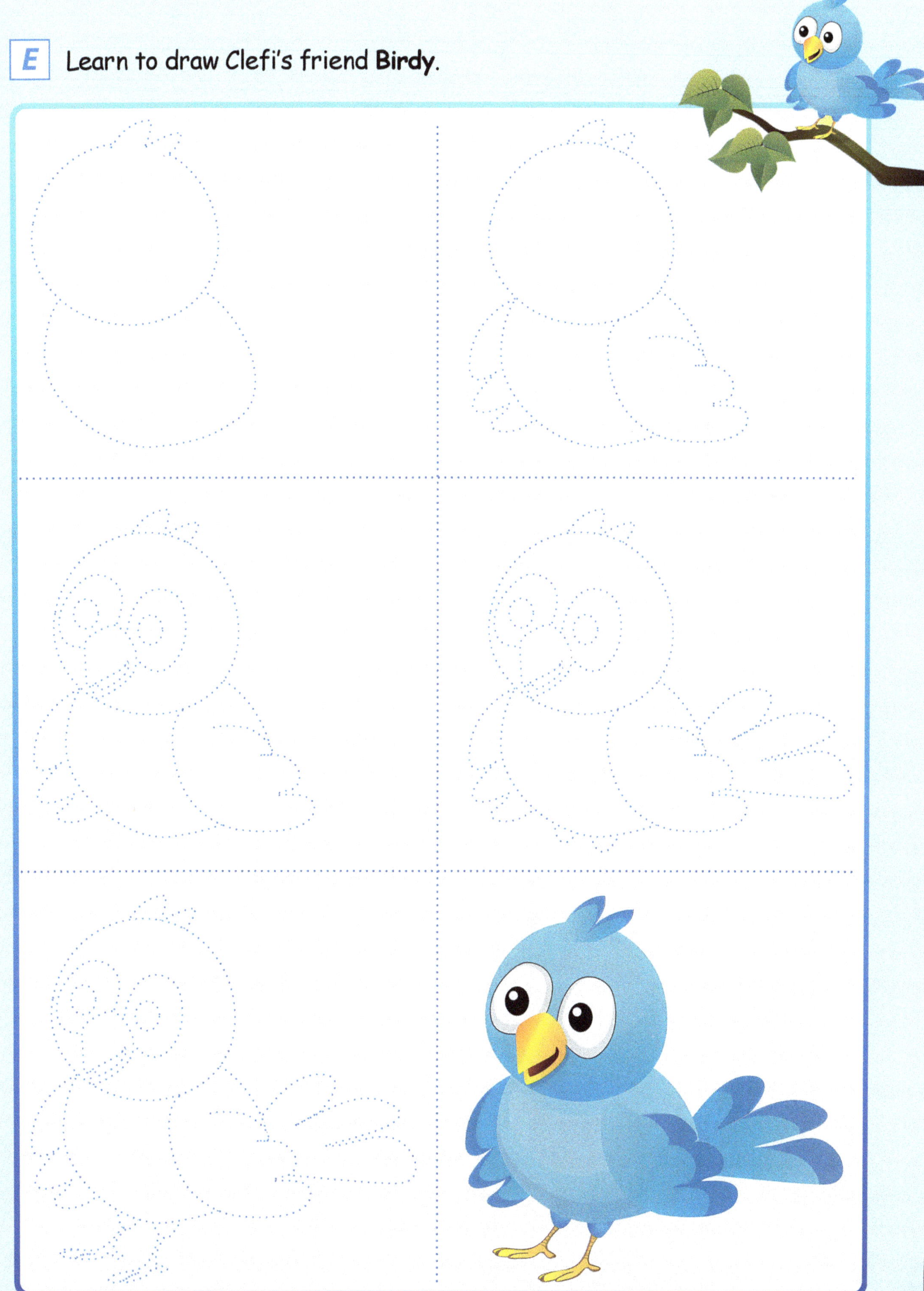

NOTE & MUSICAL STAFF

A **note** is a **musical symbol** for a **tone**, which is a **musical sound**. When writing the notes, we use the **musical staff**. The **placement** of a **note** on the **musical staff** tells us its **pitch**, which is how **high** or **low** it sounds.

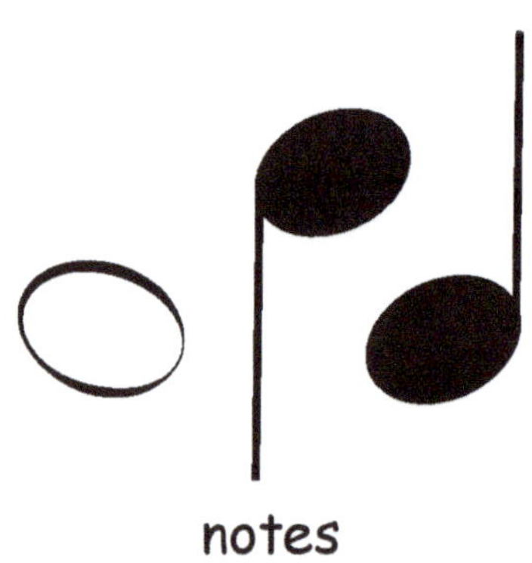

notes

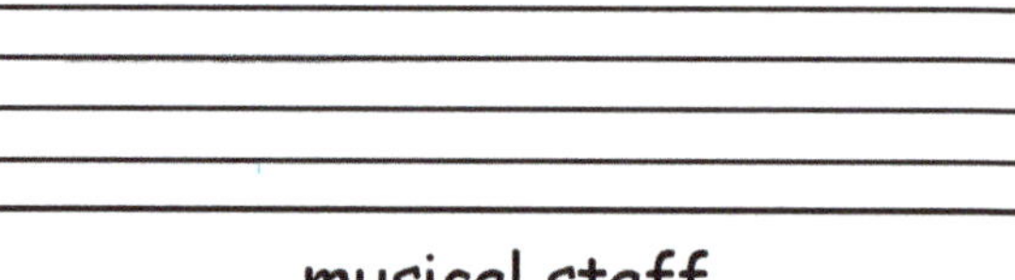

musical staff

When we write words, we write them on a line. The notes also have **staff lines**. The **staff** has **five lines**, like the fingers on a hand.

E Trace the **notes**. Do you remember **where** the **notes** belong?

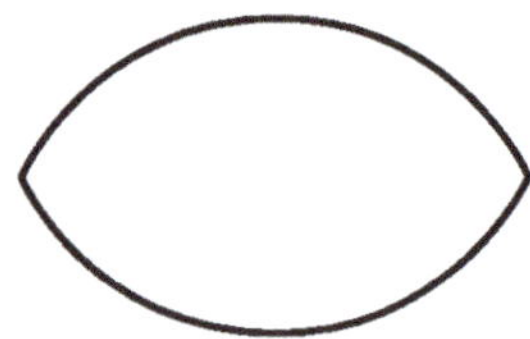

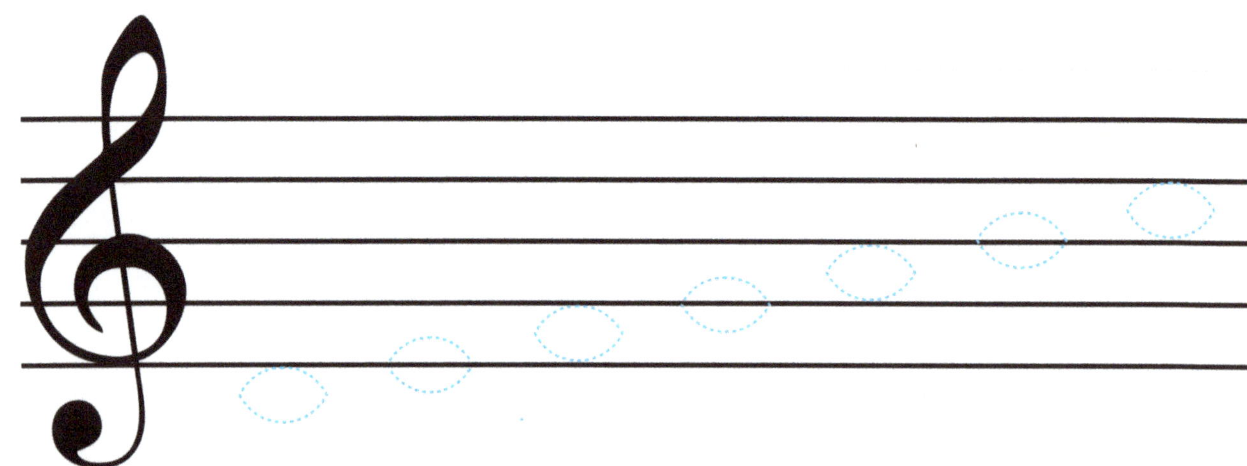

MUSICAL STAFF

The **musical staff** has **five lines** and **four spaces**.
We count them from the bottom up.

Pinky's line is the first one down
Every finger has its line
One, two, three, and four, and five
You are counting them just fine

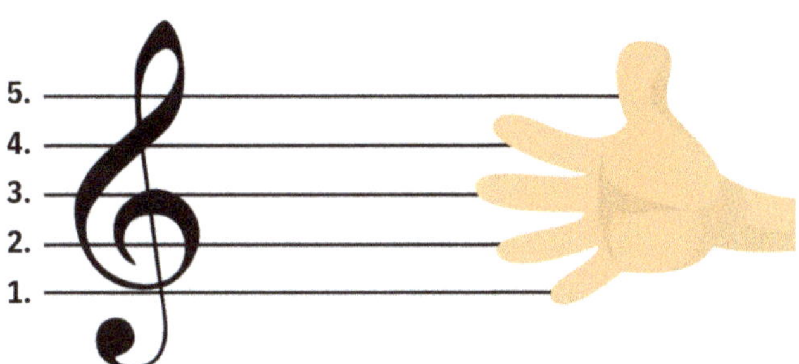

E Trace the staff **lines** with their **assigned color**.

5.
4.
3.
2.
1.

E Color the staff **spaces** with their **assigned color**.

4.
3.
2.
1.

E Trace the **lines** and color the **spaces** according to the **previous exercises**.

NOTES ON MUSICAL STAFF

On a musical staff, a note can sit:

- **on a line**

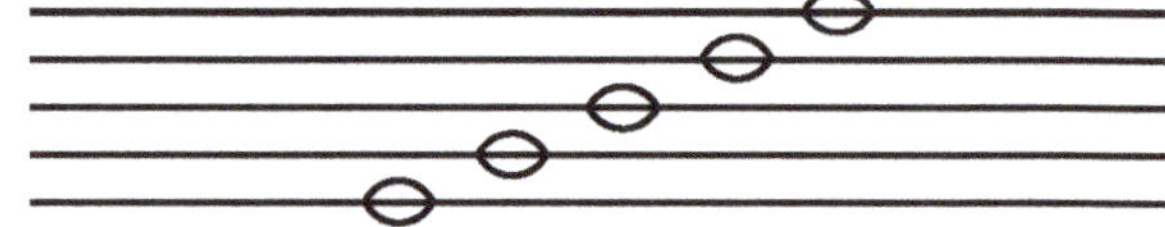

- **in a space**

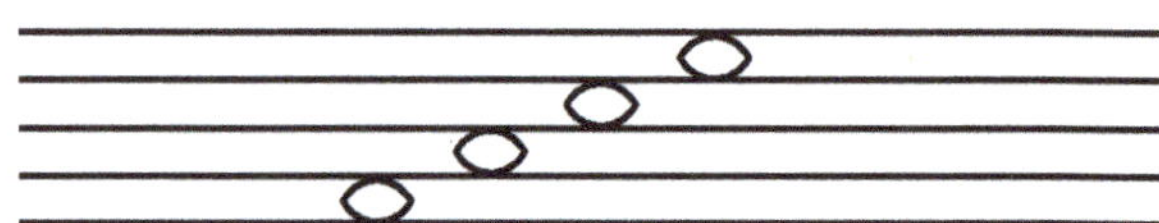

- **right below the staff**

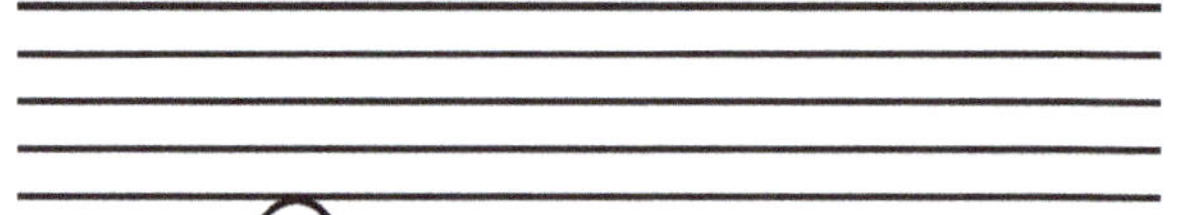

- **on the top of the staff**

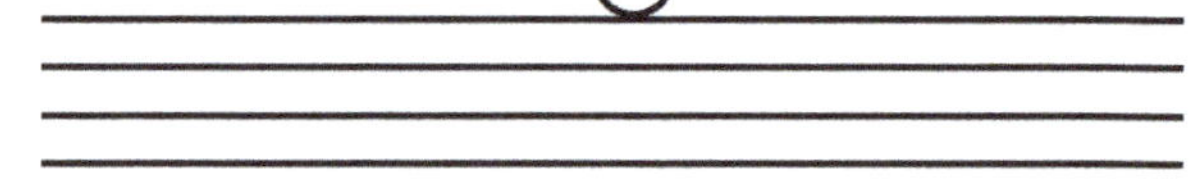

- **on a ledger line**

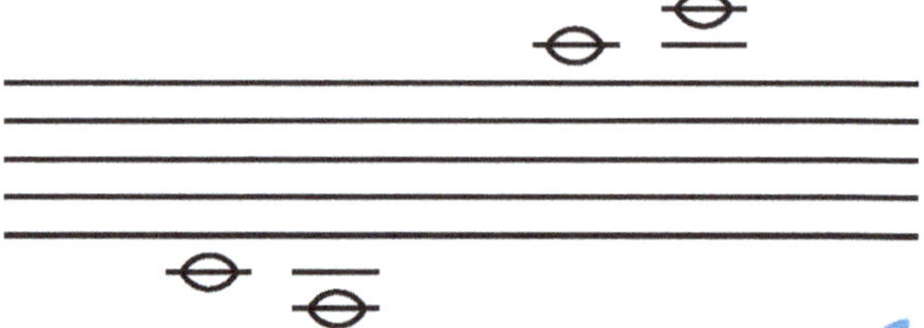

E Circle the **notes** with their **assigned colors:**

- notes **on a line** red
- notes **in a space** blue
- notes **below the staff** green
- notes **on the top of the staff** yellow
- notes **on a ledger line** brown

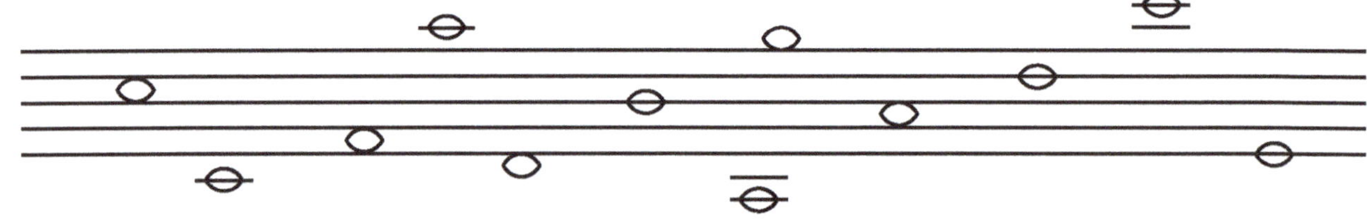

DRAWING NOTES

A note on a line:

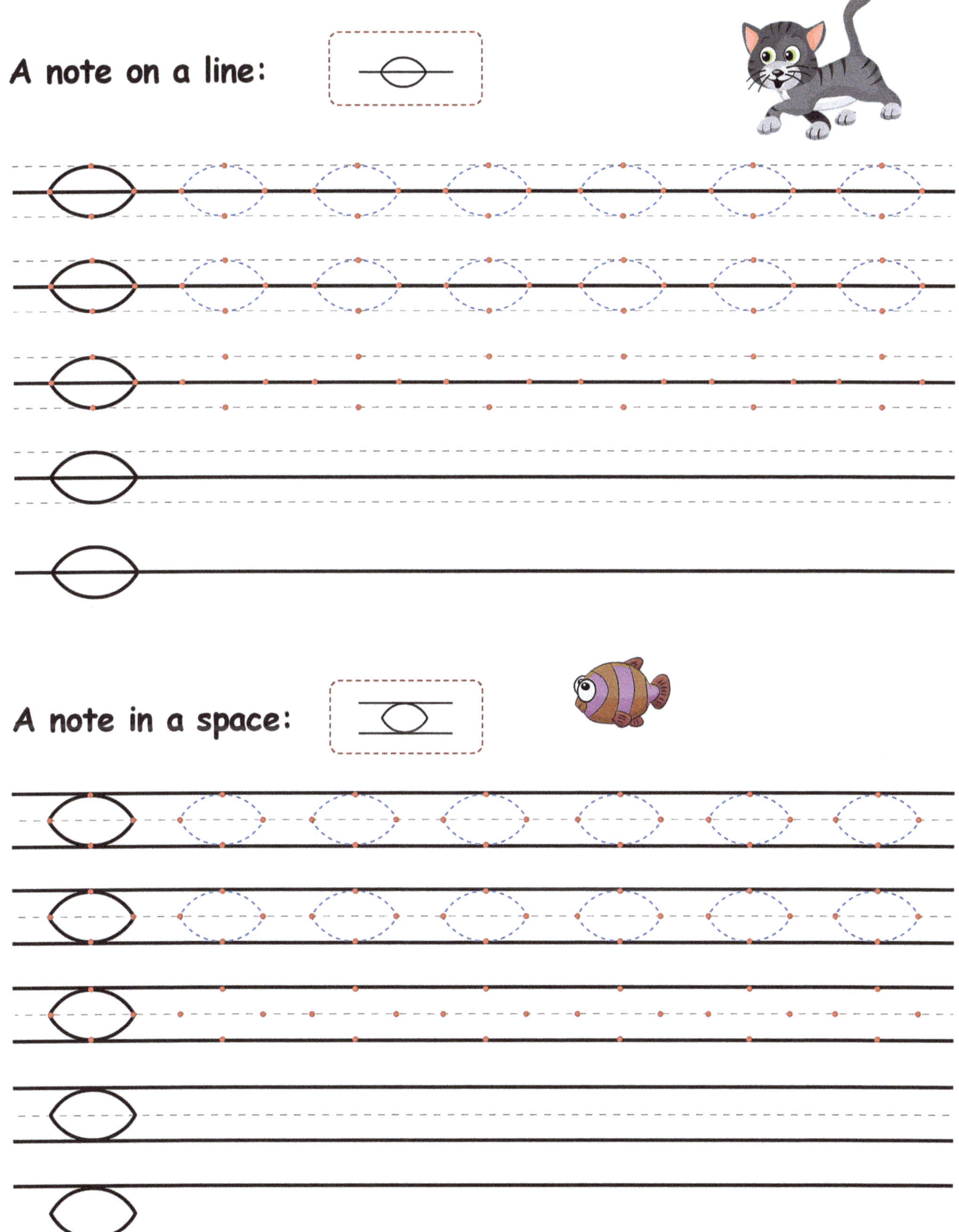

A note in a space:

CLEF

Before we can write songs on the musical staff, we must "unlock" it with a **musical clef**. The word "clef" has its root in the French word "**le clé**," which means "a key."

The **CLEF** is a symbol at the **beginning** of the **musical staff** telling us at which **register - position** we read the notes in **musical notation**.

The high notes use the **TREBLE CLEF**, also known as the **VIOLIN CLEF**. Violins play pieces written in the **treble/violin clef**.

The low notes use the **BASS CLEF**. Basses play pieces written in the **bass clef**.

E Color the butterflies with the **treble clefs** red and blue 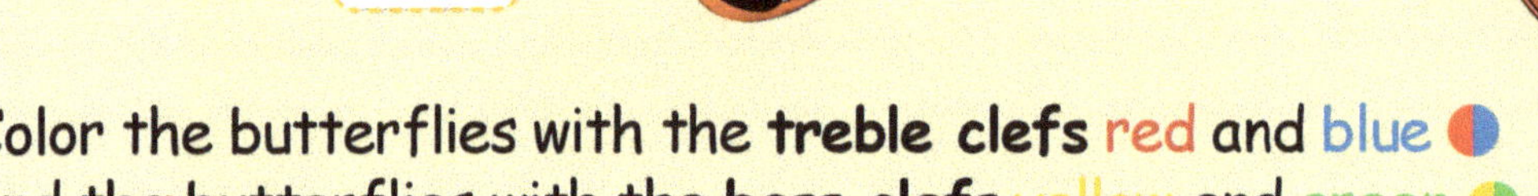 and the butterflies with the **bass clefs** yellow and green.

DRAWING TREBLE CLEF

The best-known clef, the **TREBLE CLEF**, also called the **G clef**, starts on and circles around the **second line,** marking the place of the note G4.

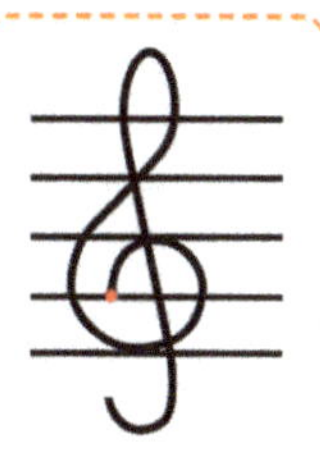

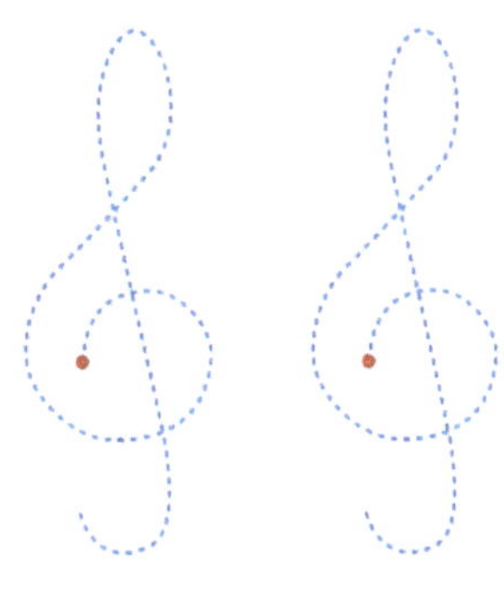

E Start by tracing the **treble clef** from the red dot and continue in one motion. Try tracing the **clefs to the left** several times, then learn to draw the treble clef by **practicing** the **smaller sections** below.

MORE ABOUT NOTES

A **NOTE** is a symbol for a **tone** = the **musical sound**. Notes have several shapes. The **shape** of the **note** tells us the **length** of the **tone** it represents. Every note has a **head**. Some notes also have a **stem,** and some also have a **flag**.

- **HEAD**

  Every note has a **head.**

  The head can be **empty** (white). Such notes are longer.

  The head can be **filled** (black). Such notes are shorter.

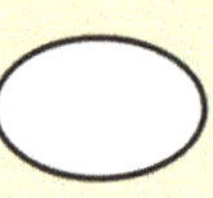

- **STEM**

  Some notes have a **stem.**

  All notes with filled heads have a **stem.**

- **FLAG** and **BEAM**

  The shortest notes have a **FLAG** that turns into a **BEAM** when we connect them.

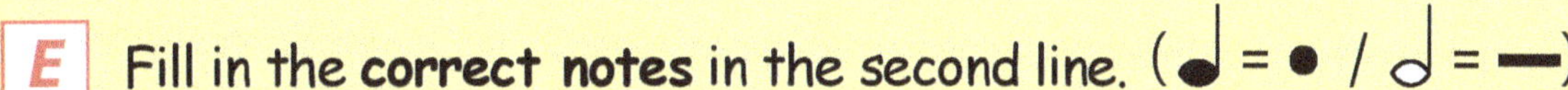

E Fill in the **correct notes** in the second line.

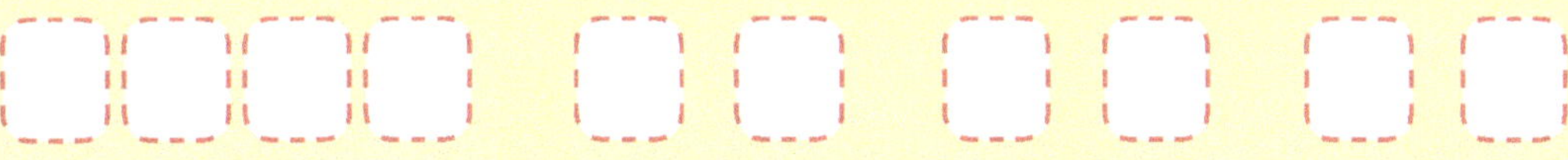

Songbook page 54

Review

yes ← empty **HEAD** filled → no

yes ← **STEM** → yes

no ← **FLAG** → yes

E Circle the **notes** with the **assigned** colors.

- with empty heads without a stem **red**
- with empty heads with a stem **blue**
- with filled heads with stems **green**
- with a flag **yellow**
- with a beam **brown**

NOTE DURATION

Notes have **various durations** and various **counts of beats**. The number of beats tells us the **note's duration**.

To understand how beats work, we will use cakes to demonstrate. The **whole cake** has **four parts**, the same as the **whole note** has **four beats**. Let's see how many smaller parts and notes we fit in.

 4 beats

THE WHOLE NOTE = THE WHOLE CAKE

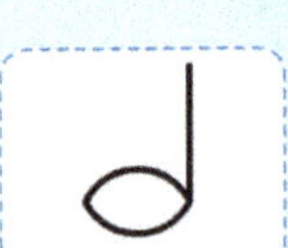 2 beats

THE HALF NOTE = THE HALF A CAKE
Two half notes (2+2 beats) = One whole note (4 beats)

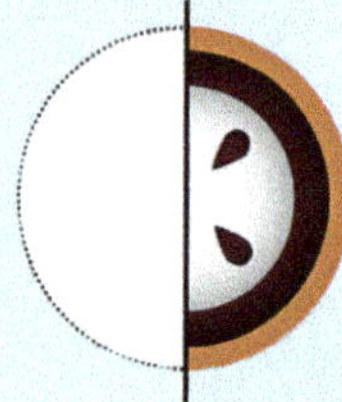

 1 beat

THE QUARTER NOTE = A QUARTER OF A CAKE
Four quarter notes (one beat each) = One whole note (4 beats)

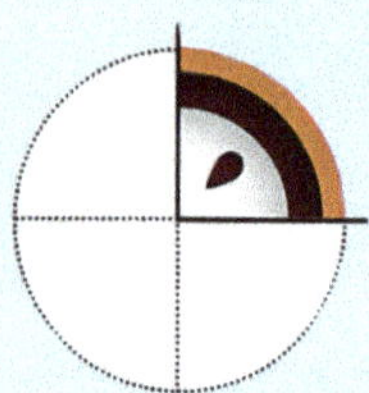

 1/2 beat

THE EIGHTH NOTE = AN EIGHTH OF A CAKE
Eight eighth notes (a half a beat each) = One whole note (4 beats)

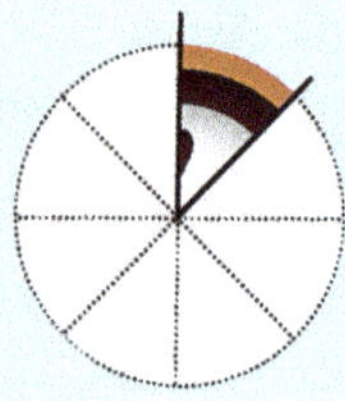

E Write the **correct number** of beats for each **note** into the **box next to it**.

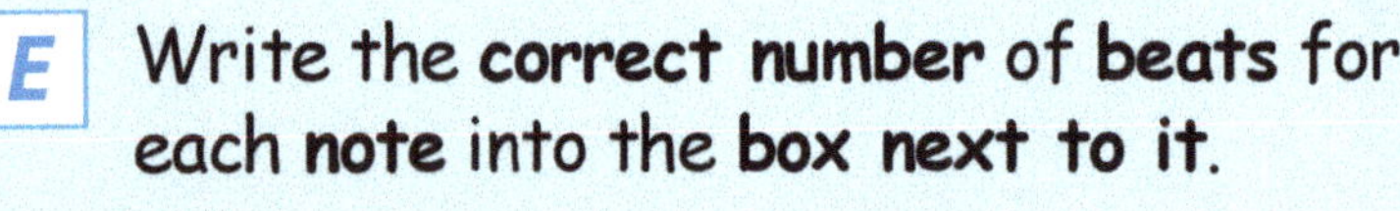

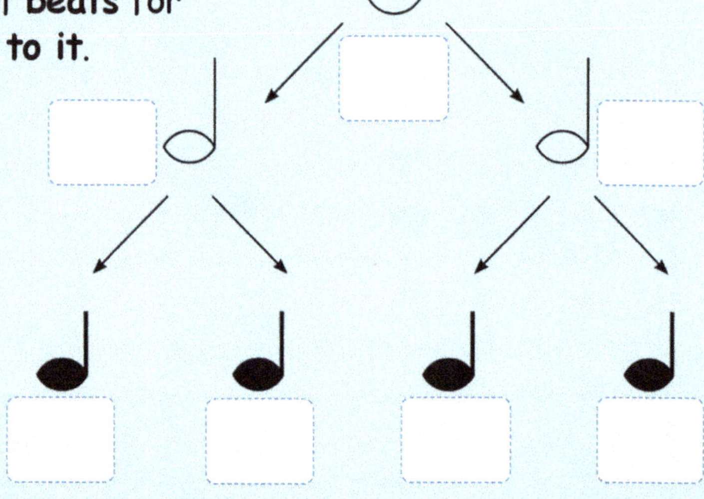

DRAWING STEMS & FLAGS

Stems are attached to the notes:

- **upwards** on the note's **right side**
- **downwards** on the note's **left side**

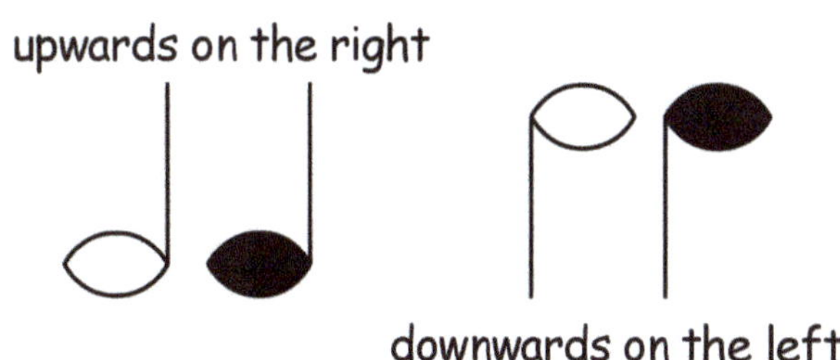

A **half note** has an empty head and a stem.

A **quarter note** has a full head and a stem.

E Draw **half** notes and **quarter** notes on the **line** and in the **space**.

An **eighth note** has a full head, a stem, and a flag.

E Practice drawing the **flag** as if you were drawing a part of a **leaf**.

NOTES WITH STEM

● In the **bottom part** of the **staff**, up to the **middle line**, we draw notes with the **stem upwards** on the **right side** of the **note**.

E Practice drawing notes with **stems upward**.

● In the **top part** of the **staff**, from the **middle line** up, we draw notes with the stem **downwards** on the **left side** of the **note**

E Practice drawing notes with **stems downward**.

● On the **middle line**, the **third line** of the **staff**, we can draw notes with **stems** on **either side** of the **note** with the **correct direction**.

E Draw a **treble clef** and add the **correct stems** to the **notes**.

RESTS

The **RESTS** are musical symbols for silence.
They tell us how long we **shouldn't sing** or **play**.
Rests have the same names as their note siblings.

Whole Rest	Half Rest	Quarter Rest	Eighth Rest
four beats	two beats	one beat	half a beat

E Draw the **rests** according to the examples. Watch out for the **difference** between the **whole** rest and the **half** rest. They have the **same shape**, but each is **placed differently** on a **different line** of the staff.

The **whole rest** is **four** beats long and **hangs down** from the **fourth line**.
The **half rest** is **two** beats long and **sits on** the **third line**.

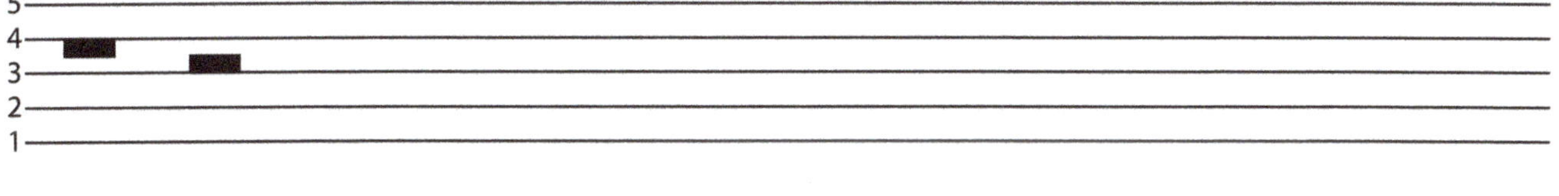

The **quarter rest** looks like a fancy **lightning bolt**.

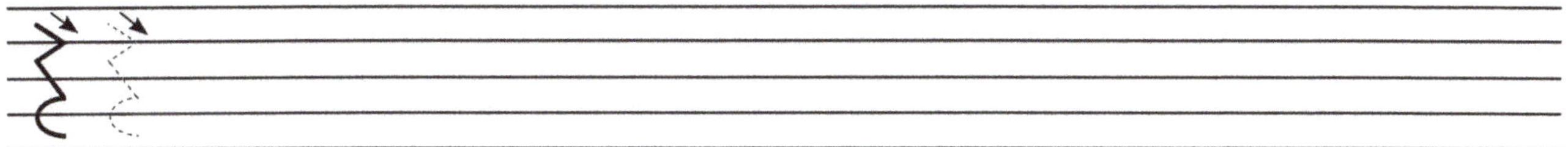

The **eighth rest** is quite simple and starts on the **fourth line**.

E **Connect** the **flowers with rests** with the correct **numbered flowers**.

MEASURE & TIME SIGNATURE

On the **staff**, the notes of a song are **organized** into **small boxes**, like letters grouped into words. These boxes are called **measures**. The **measures** are separated by lines. These lines are called the **measure lines** or **bar lines**.

- The **MEASURES** are small sections of a musical piece separated by the **MEASURE LINES**.

To ensure we know **how many notes** and **how long** we can place in a measure, we use the **time signature** or **meter**.

- The **TIME SIGNATURE** is a numeric sign made of **two numbers** on **top** of **each other**. It's placed at the **beginning** of a piece, right **after** the **clef**. It tells us how to **count** individual **measures**.

E Color the flowers that mark the **measures** red●.
Color the flowers that mark the measure lines blue●.
Circle the **time signature** in green○.

RAIN IS FALLING Songbook page 55

When we clap evenly while singing, we are clapping the **beats**.
When we can count all the beats in the song like:
one-two-three-four, one-two-three-four, ...
or
one-two-three, one-two-three, ...
means that all **measures** in the song have the **same amount of beats**.

The **TIME SIGNATURE** shows
the **number of beats** per measure and the **note value**.

The **THREE-FOUR MEASURE**
is marked with the numbers **3/4**. The measure
has three beats, and the beat is a **quarter note**.
We count it **one-two-three**.

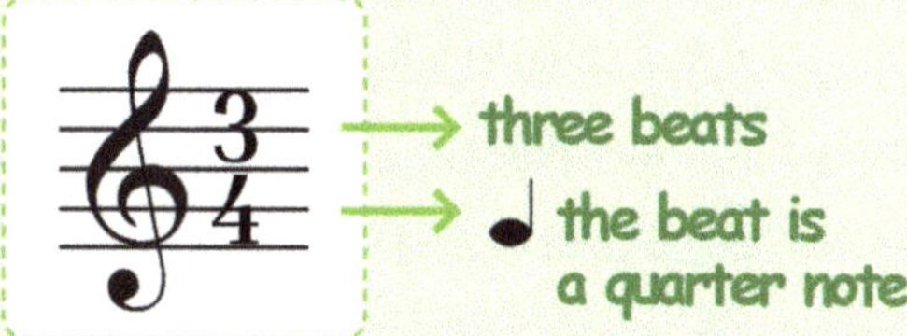

The **FOUR-FOUR MEASURE** or the **COMMON
METER** is marked with the numbers **4/4** or with
the capital letter C. The measure has **four
beats**, and the **beat** is a **quarter note**.
We count it **one-two-three-four**.

E Learn the **songs** from Clefi's Songbook. **Sing** and **count** the **beats** out loud.
Mark the **beats** with **dots** under the notes and write down the **number** of
beats in each **measure**.

RHYTHM & DOWNBEATS

When we **clap while singing**, we naturally **feel** some **beats** to be **more important**. We call these beats the HEAVY BEATS.
You may notice that we naturally want to make the **heavy beats** more present, like with **stomping** or **louder clapping**.

The clearest **heavy beats** are on the **first beats** of measures. We call these beats the **DOWNBEATS**. The **heavy** and **light beats** in the measure help us tell if the song is in **3/4** or **4/4 meter** - its **RHYTHM**.

E Sing the song "Cat is Coming Down" twice, **clapping** the **rhythm** following the dots and dashes. The second time through, **stomp** on every **downbeat**.

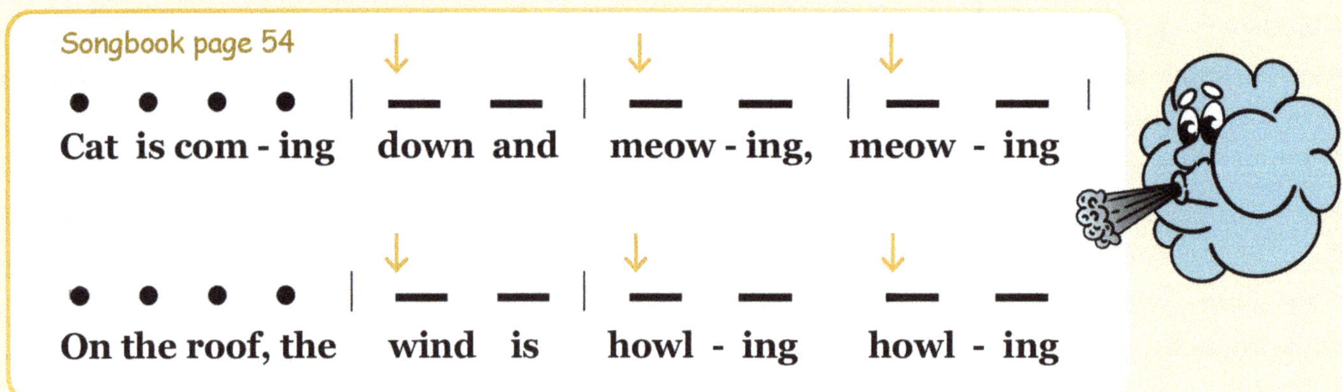

E Clap the **rhythm** of the songs, and mark the **downbeats** with the blue arrow ↓.
Write the **correct** 3/4 or 4/4 **meter** into the frames before each song.

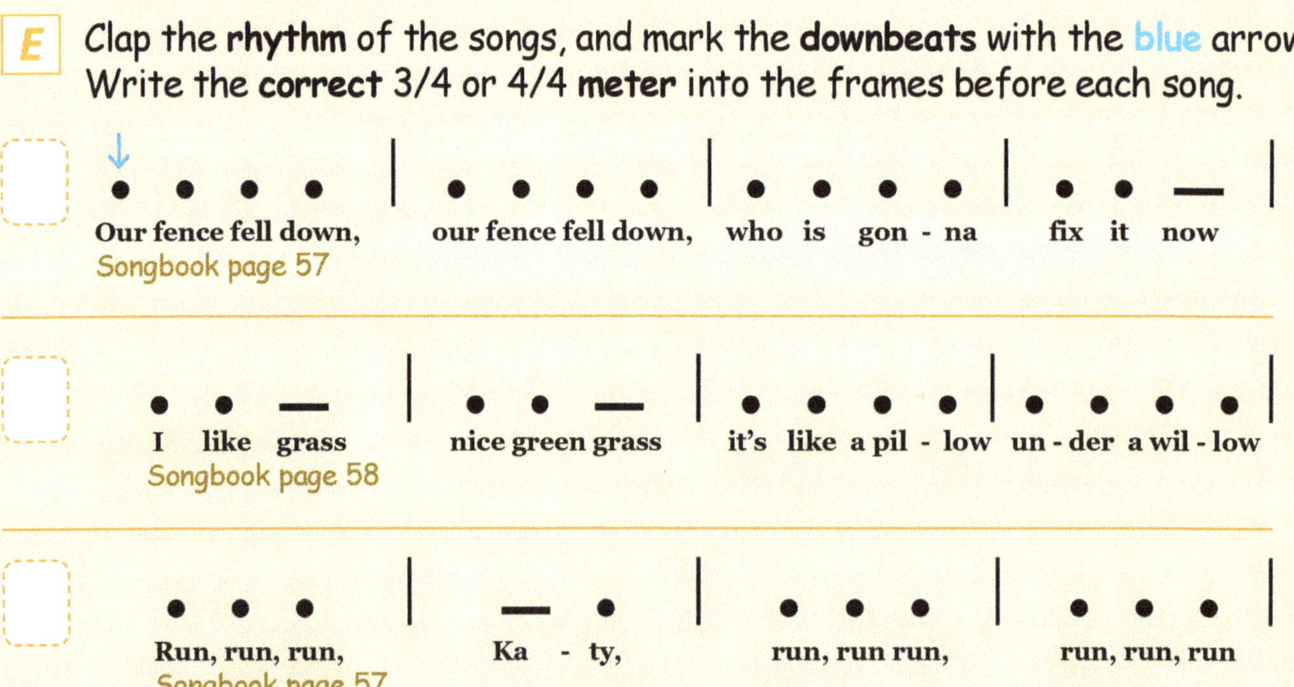

CLEFI'S LITTLE REVIEW

- The **NOTE** is a musical symbol for a tone.
- The **REST** is a musical symbol for silence.

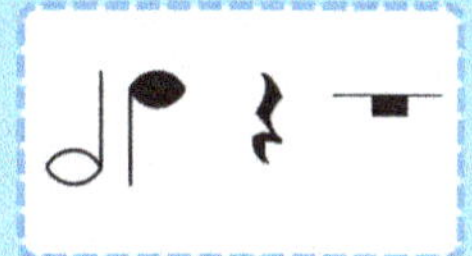

- The **MUSICAL STAFF** has **five lines** and **four spaces**. We use the staff to write down the notes.
- Before we start writing the notes on the staff, we have to open it with the **CLEF**.

- The **MEASURE** is a section of a musical piece separated by the **MEASURE LINES**.
- The **TIME SIGNATURE** tells us the number of beats in a measure and the note value of a beat.

E Color the buterflies:
- the one with the notes
- the one with the rests
- the one with the staff
- the one with the clefs
- the one with the meter

MUSICAL ALPHABET

The **MUSICAL ALPHABET** has only **seven letters**,
which we use to name the tones and notes.
Those seven tones create the **primary tone row**.

C D E F G A B

PIANO KEYBOARD

Let's see where these notes live on the **piano keyboard**.
Every note has its little room - a **key**. The **keys** are **white** and
black. The **primary tone row** is played on the **white keys** only.

The **black keys** are organized in **groups** of **two** and **three**, with
a white key in between each black key. Two white keys
separate the groups. The first primary note, *C*, lives **right**
below the **group** of **two black keys**.

E Write the correct **names** of the **notes** into the **circles** on the **keys**.

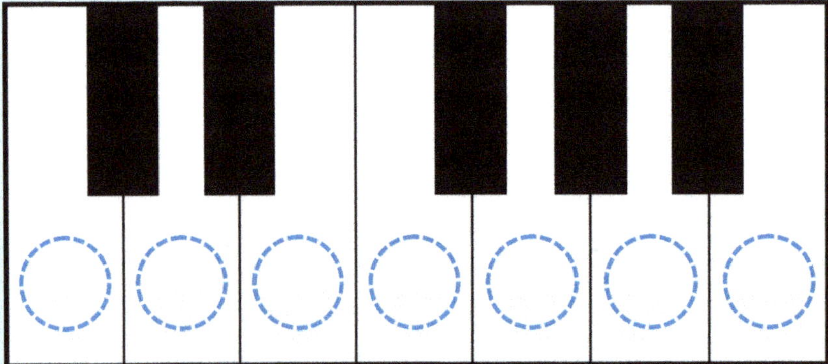

OCTAVES

On the keyboard, the **primary tone row** CDEFGAB repeats several times at different **heights**. The tone **C** with its new row keeps coming back right after the last note **B**.

To keep the notes organized, we group them into the **OCTAVES**. Each new **OCTAVE** that starts with the note **C** has its own **number**.

The children mostly sing in the **middle octave**, which starts with the note **C4** - the **middle C**. All the notes in the middle octave have number **4** - C4 D4 E4 F4 G4 A4 B4 .

The **octaves** are numbered from the **lowest** to the **highest**, with the **lowest** being the **first octave** or **octave 1**.

E Fill in the **names** of the **missing notes**, including the correct **octave number**. Follow the sections on the snails's house in precise order.

HALF STEPS & WHOLE STEPS

Some white keys **do not have** a black key between them.
These keys are E and F and B and C.
Let's see it on the piano keyboard.

- The **HALF STEP** is the **smallest distance** between the two tones. It does not matter if the keys are **both white** or **mixed**.

- The **WHOLE STEP** contains **two half steps**. When the two neighboring white keys have a black key between them, the distance between the two white keys is a **whole step**. The **grouped black keys** have white keys between each black key, so they are **all** a **whole step apart**.

E Show the pairs of tones below on the keyboard. Can you tell which are a **half step** and which a **whole step** apart? Color the squares with the notes above them a half step apart red and a whole step apart green.

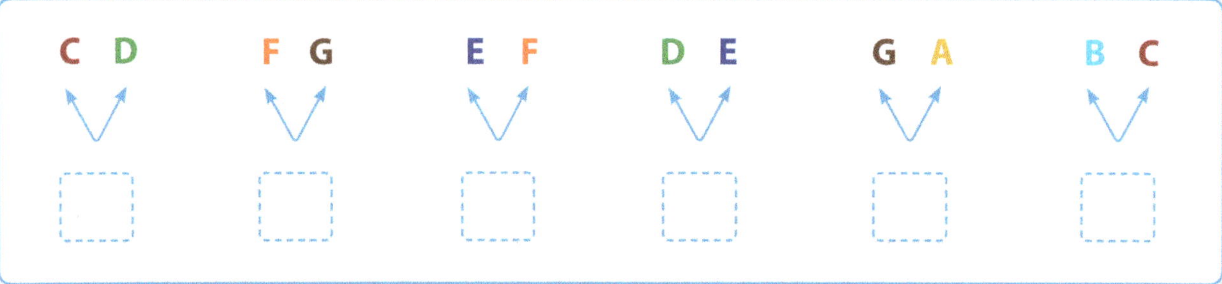

C MAJOR SCALE

The tones **C D E F G A B C** make a **tone row** we call a **SCALE**. A **scale starts** and **ends** with the **same tone** exactly **one octave (eight tones) apart**.

The **C MAJOR SCALE** is made of the tones of the **primary row**. It starts and ends with the tone C.
The low C and high C are **one octave apart**.

E Write the names of the **C Major scale** notes on the keyboard. Color the **keys** with a **half step** between them **yellow**.

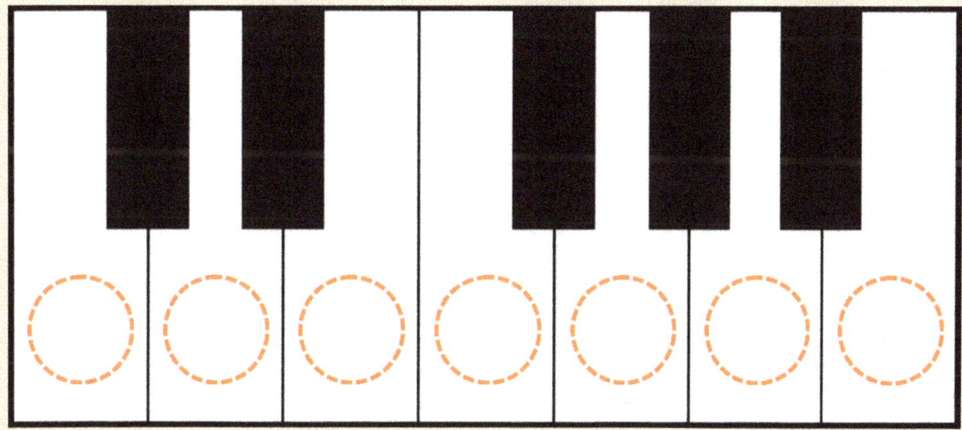

E Let's learn "The C Major Song" so that we can remember the notes of the **C Major scale** better.

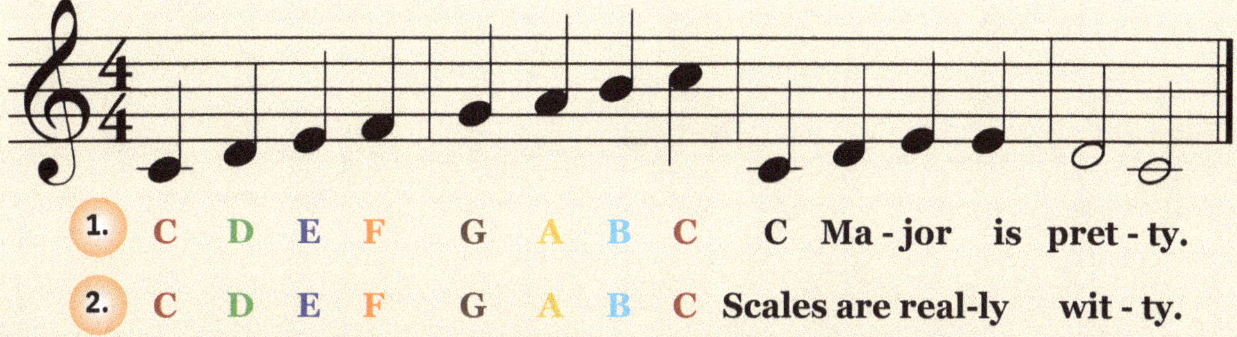

FUN WITH C MAJOR SCALE

Now that we can sing the complete scale, it's time to learn how to notate it on the musical staff and read it from there. Picture the staff as power lines, with the notes resembling small birds perched on them or fluttering between them. Below the lines, there's a charming little house with a pebble-covered path leading up to it.

Imagine the road leading to the house. But it's not just any road because it's covered with pebbles. That's why we call it the **COVERED Road - C.**

C - Covered Road

The note on the first ledger line below the staff.

The little house sits right at the end of the road. It's literally a little house **DOWN** the Covered Road.

D - down the road

The note right below the staff.

One little swalow sits on each of the first three lines.

E - Ellen

The note on the first line.

G - Gaby

The note on the second line.

B - Betty

The note on the third line.

One little robin flutters in each the bottom three spaces .

F - Frank

The note in the first space.

A - Adam

The note in the second space.

C - Charlie

The note in the third space.

WRITING DOWN C MAJOR SCALE

On the staff, the notes are lined up in a tone row
C D E F G A B C like on the keyboard.

In the treble clef, the note **C4** sits on the **first ledger line below the staff**.
The other notes line up in a row, consistently one place higher,
alternating between the lines and spaces.

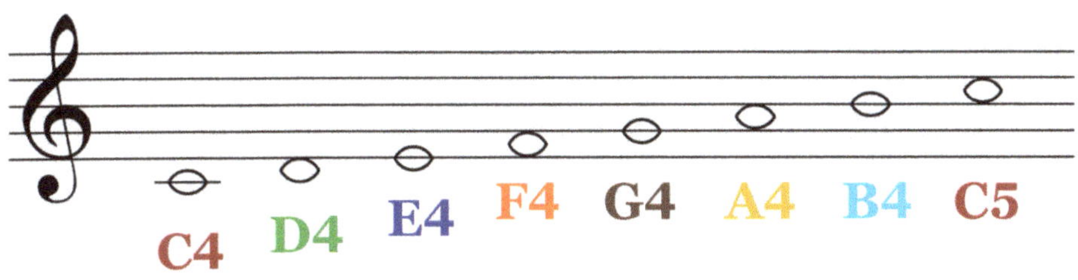

E   Fill the **names** of the **notes** into the **squares**.

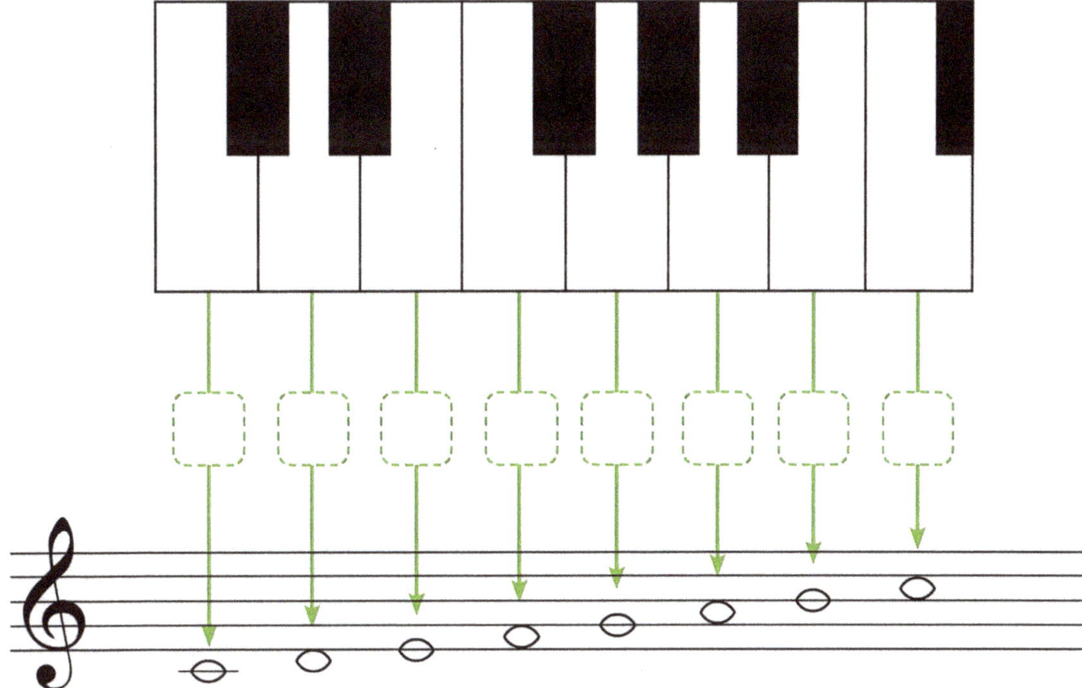

E   Draw the **treble clef** and the **C Major scale**.

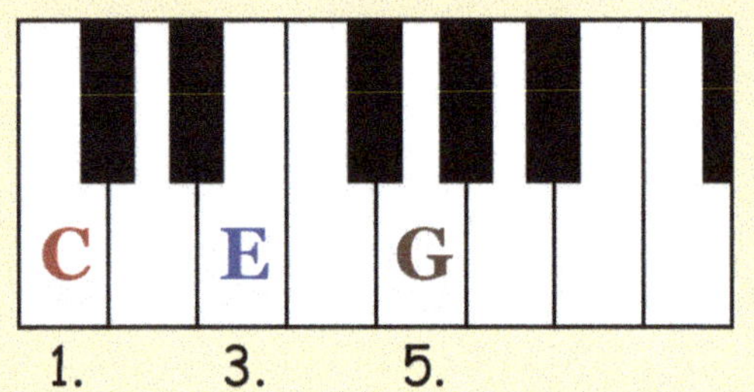

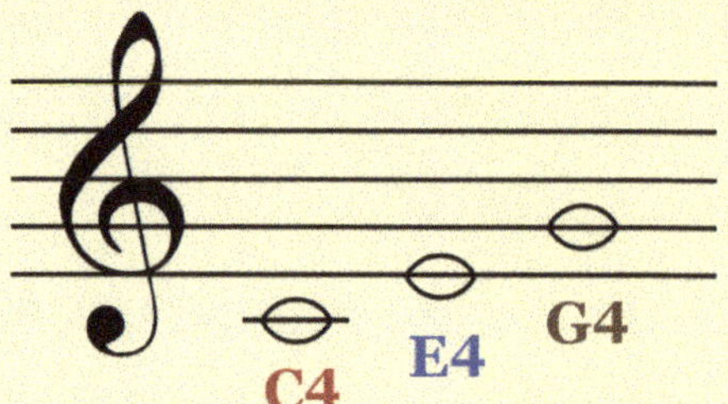

Any scale's **first**, **third**, and **fifth** tones are its **SUPPORT TONES**.

E Sing the **C Major scale** and write the **names** of the notes into the squares.

1. 3. 5.

E Draw the **notes** according to the example.

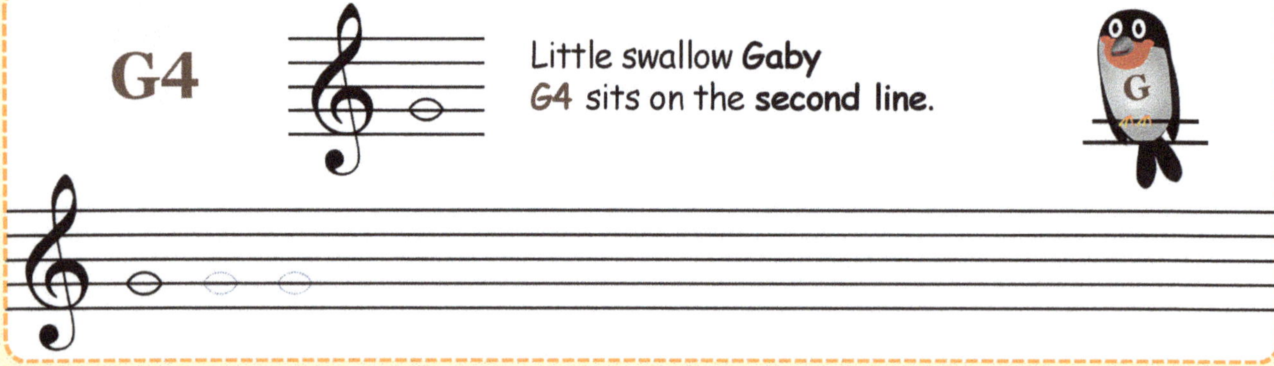

SUBSTITUTE MUSICAL STAFF

One of our hands will be our **substitute musical staff**.
The other hand will point to where the notes sit.

Let's point at the notes C4, E4, and G4.

 You already know the following songs. Can you **sing** them using the **notes' names**? Point at your **fingers**, using your hand as a **substitute staff**.

 Learn the new song, sing it using **notes' names**, and show them on your **hand**. Then, circle the notes C4 maroon, E4 dark blue, and G4 brown.

LITTLE CUCKOO BIRD   Songbook page 59

NOTES D4, F4, AND A4

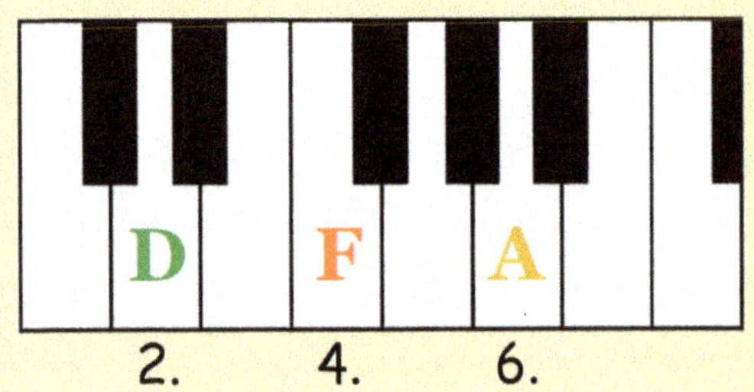

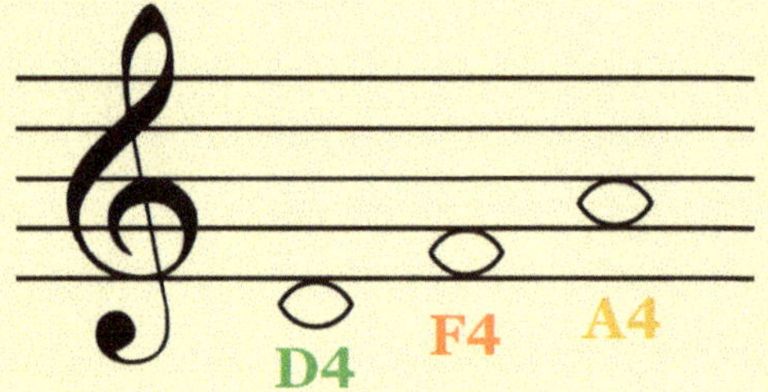

E Draw the **notes** according to the example.

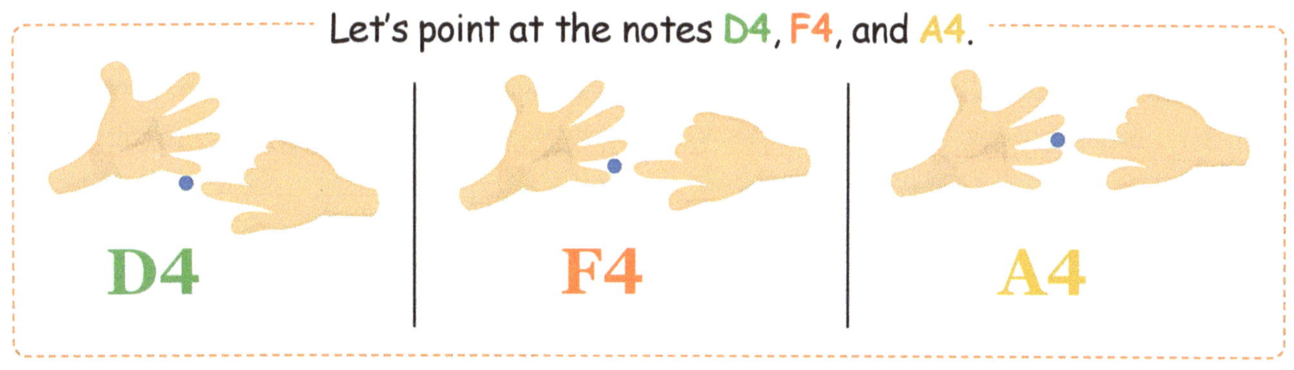

E Circle the notes D4 green, E4 orange, and A4 golden yellow.

BOO HID UNDER A FENCE Songbook page 53

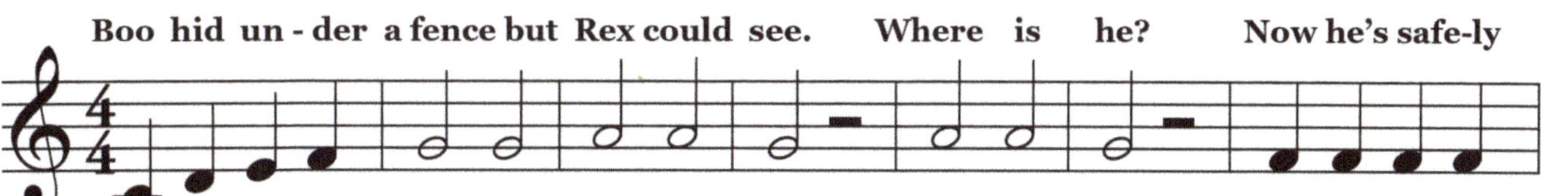

E Learn the new song from the Songbook.
Write down the **name** of the **notes** on the line.

How **many** of these
notes are in the **song**?

WE ARE LITTLE MUSICIANS Songbook page 59

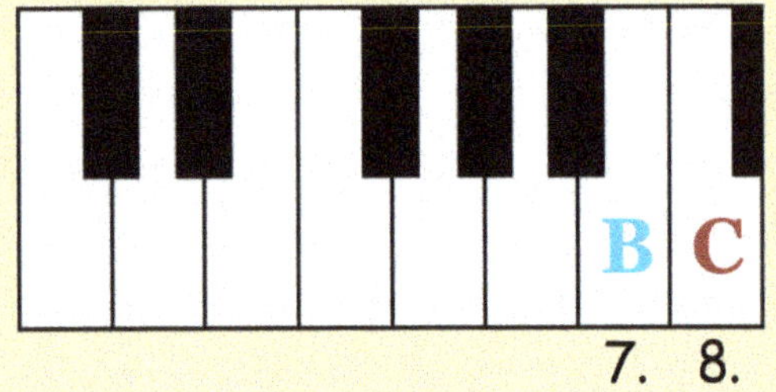

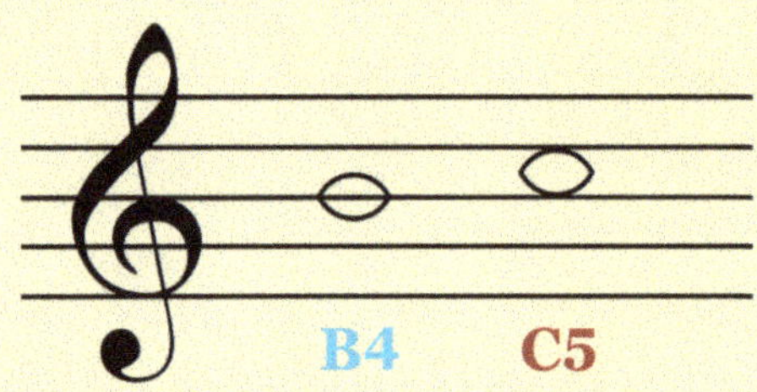

E Draw the **notes** according to the example.

E Write the **names** of the notes.   Draw the **notes** above their names.

Find the note B4 and circle it light blue, then C5 and circle it maroon.

HEY-HO, LITTLE SHEEP *Songbook page 56*

E

1. Find the measure with the note **C5** and **copy** it on the **staff**.

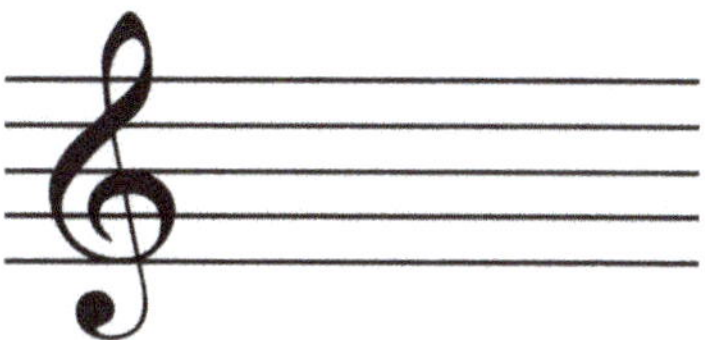

2. Read the song using the **names** of the **notes**.

3. Write the **names** of the **notes** on the lines below the staffs.

4. What is the letter **C** behind the treble clef?

5. How many **half notes** are in the song

6. How many **beats** are in the measure?

LITTLE TURTLE DOVE *Songbook page 60*

she woke up my   blue-eyed love, did - n't care that she woke up my blue-eyed love

CLEFI'S BIG REVIEW

Let's review what we've learned with Clefi so far. And do not forget to color your correct answers!

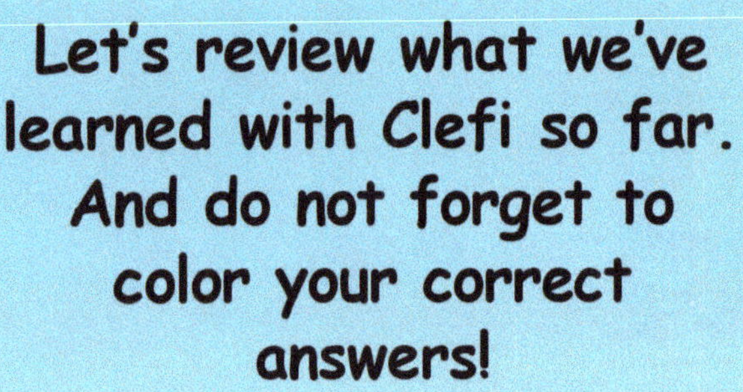

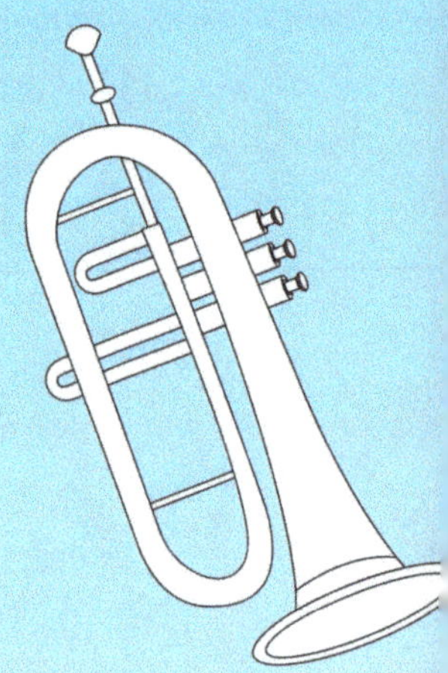

E Clap the **song** and guess its **name**.

E What makes the **ordinary** and what **musical** sound?

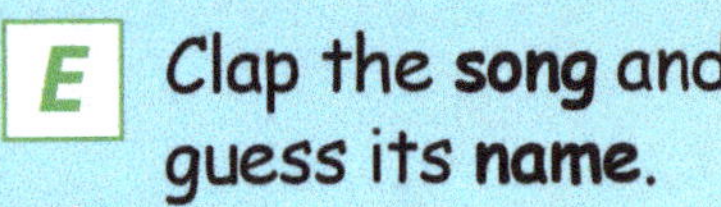

E Who is singing **tones** and who **lyrics**?

Fill in the missing letters to get the names of the notes and rests.

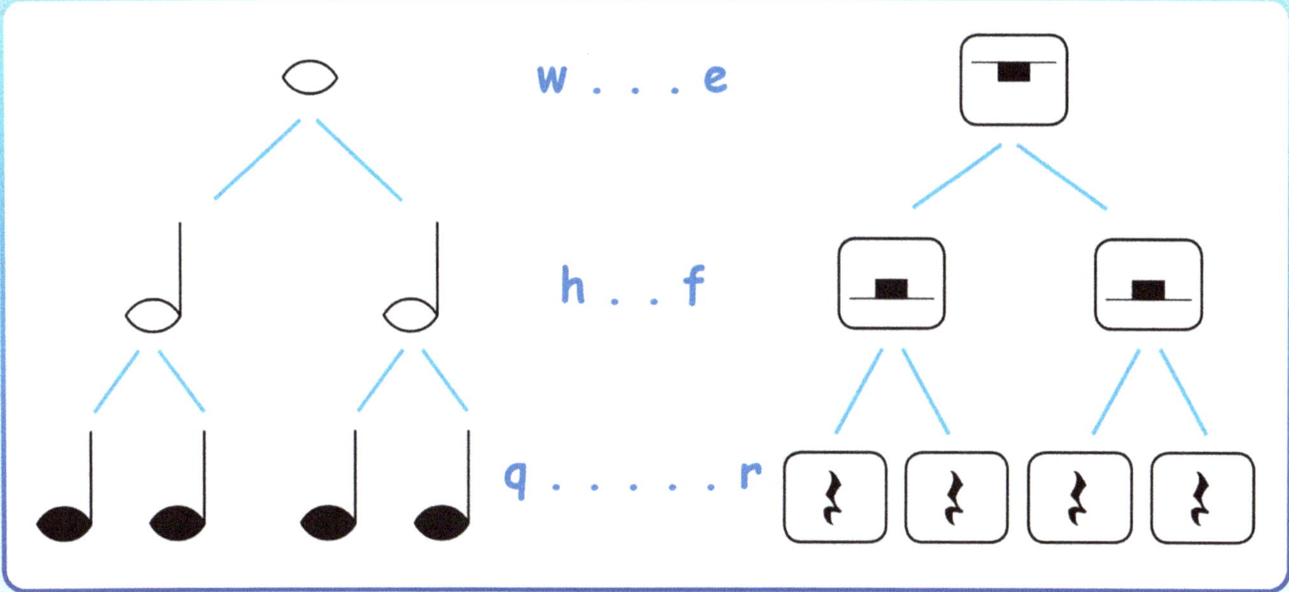

● Color the circles with **whole notes** and **whole rests** green.
● Color the circles with **half notes** and **half rests** yellow.
● Color the circles with **quarter notes** and **quarter rests** blue.

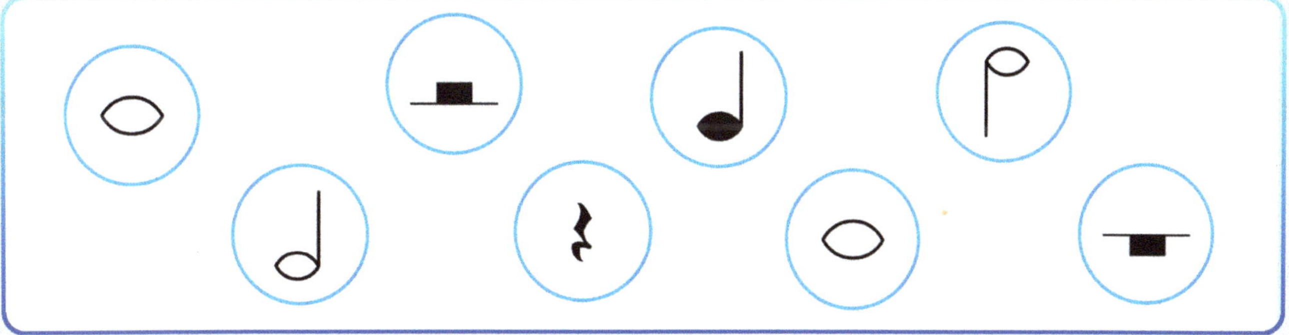

Write a dot ● under the quarter notes, a dash ▬ under the half notes, and the square with the quarter rest leave empty.

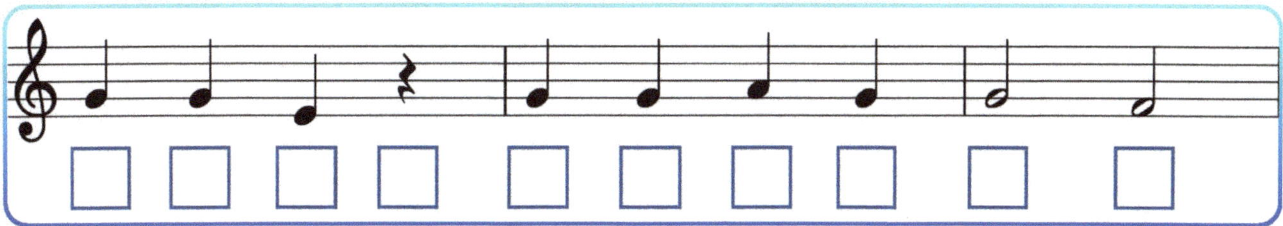

NOTE / REST / STAFF / CLEF / METER

E Color the buterflies:

- the one with the notes yellow
- the one with the rests green
- the one with the staff blue
- the one with the clefs red
- the one with the meter orange

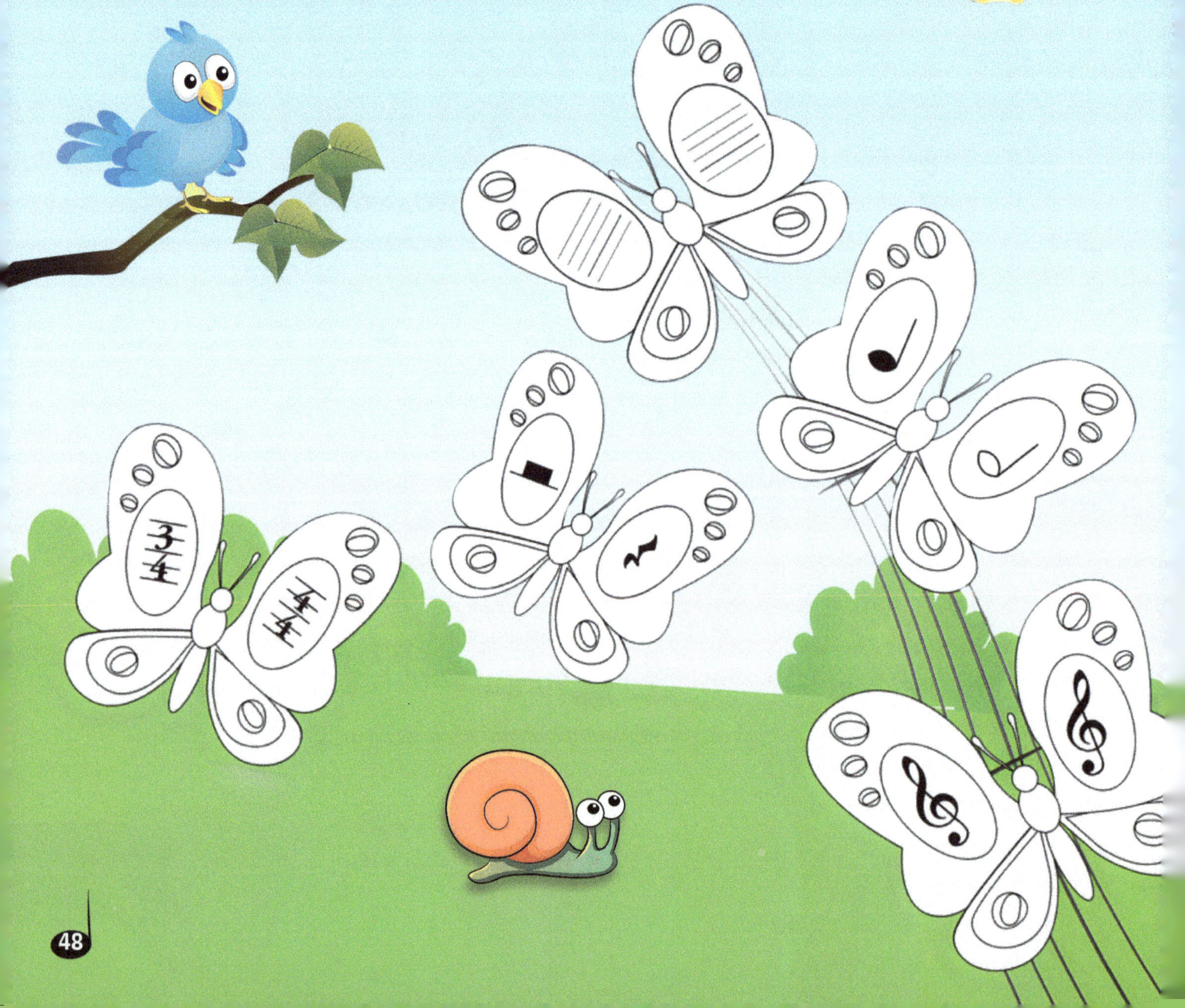

Sing or play both songs (*pages 53, 62*) and then do the exercises.
1. Do you recognize the songs? Write their **name** on the lines above them.
2. Write the **correct meter sign** - C or **3/4** - behind the treble clef.
3. Write the **names** of the **notes** on the blue lines below the staffs.
4. Write the **number** of **silent beats** under every rest sign.

1.

2.

Fill in the measure lines in the section of the song *Little Vixen, Run!*

Songbook page 54

ADDITIONAL FACTS

A SOUND travels through the air. Sound is born through vibrations.
ORDINARY SOUNDS - **noise** - are born through uneven vibrations.
MUSICAL SOUNDS or TONES are born through even vibrations.

A FOLK SONG originates from the people, and we do not know its author. It is preserved through oral transmission, such as when mothers sing to their children before bedtime, when people sing while working, or during long winter evenings when there is no TV to watch. Every song has lyrics and melody. Children's folk songs, with their simple, relatable themes, often feature animals. Today, children can learn from these simple folk songs by listening to the music and the lyrics and trying to understand their meaning. Some are just plain funny and silly, like *Little Vixen, Run!*

A folk song may change or be forgotten as it is passed down through generations. To preserve the song accurately, it should be written down. To correctly write down a song, there are certain things we need:

NOTES - A note is a **musical symbol** for a **tone**. Every note has its specific look that tells us its length. The placement of a note on the musical staff tells us how high or low it is = its pitch.

RESTS - A rest is a **musical symbol** for **silence** in music. Its shape and placement in the staff tell us how long we shouldn't sing or play.

MUSICAL CLEFS - A clef is a **musical symbol** that dictates the pitch of the notes on the staff. We write it at the beginning of the staff. The most common musical clef is the **treble clef**. We use it to write down melodies for songs and high-pitched instruments, like violins. Low voices and bass instruments like double basses use the **bass clef**.

STAFFS (STAVES) - A staff has five lines with four spaces. We use the staff to write notes on its lines and into its spaces. The staff can have more short lines above and below for individual notes. We call those lines the **ledger lines**.

MEASURES, MEASURE LINES, and TIME SIGNATURES (METERS) - In musical notation, compositions are divided into **measures**, which are small segments separated by vertical lines called **measure lines**. These measure lines are evenly spread across the staff. The length of each measure and the position of the lines are determined by the **time signature**, also known as the meter. The time signature is a **musical symbol** consisting of two numbers stacked on top of each other. These numbers indicate how **many beats** are in each measure and the **value of each beat**.

CLEFI'S SONGBOOK

Clefi loves to sing children's folk songs. Most of them are fun little tunes about animals. Some describe funny situations, like the one about the fence that fell and nobody knew how to fix it. Others are about feelings, like the one about the green grass. The most important thing is that Clefi loves to share them with you and hopes you will like them and sing them with him.

Little Sheep, Not a Peep!
Pages - 8, 9, 41

On The Tree, Our Pear Tree

Pages - 8, 31, 41

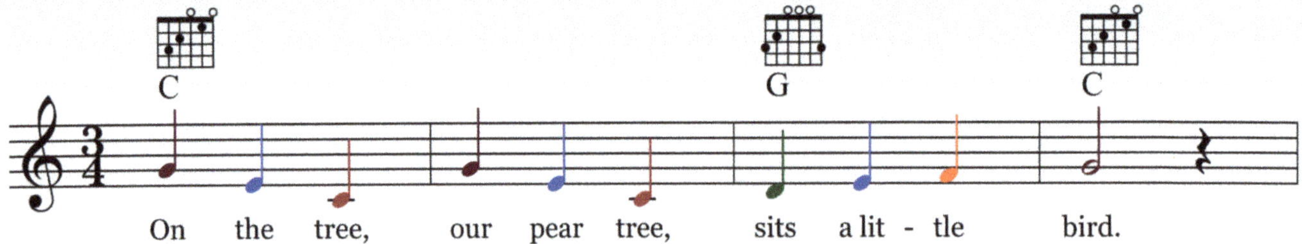

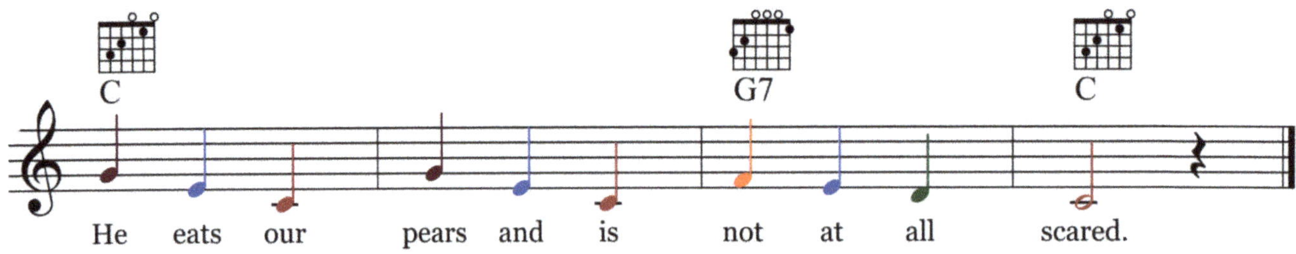

Go to Sleep, My Little Starlight

Pages - 8, 31

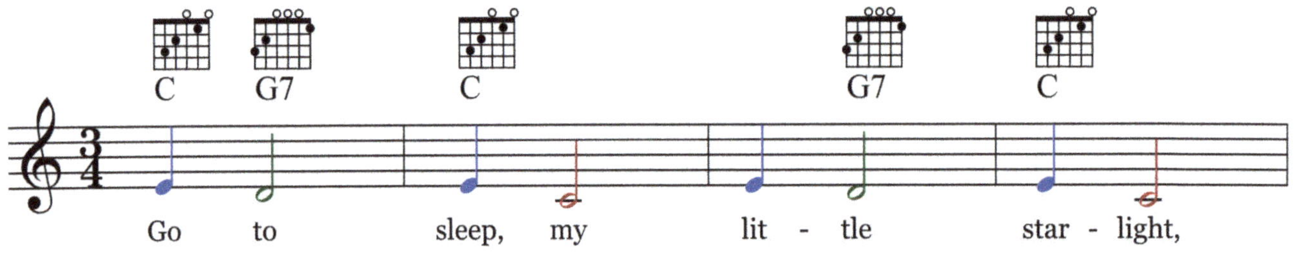

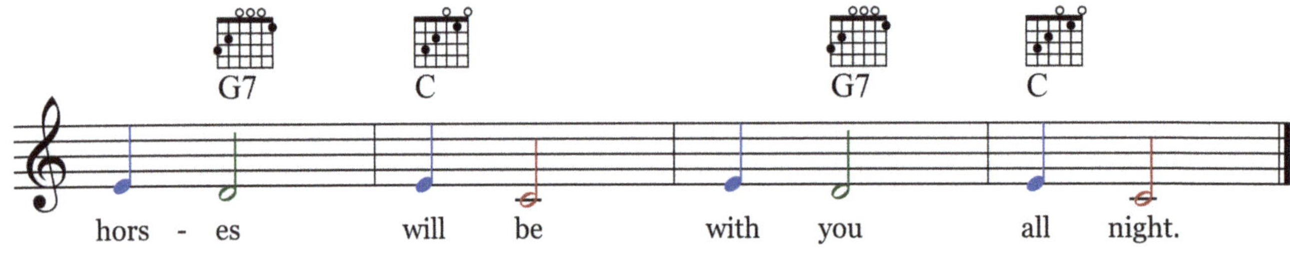

A Cat (Boo) Hid Under a Fence
Pages - 8, 11, 13, 43

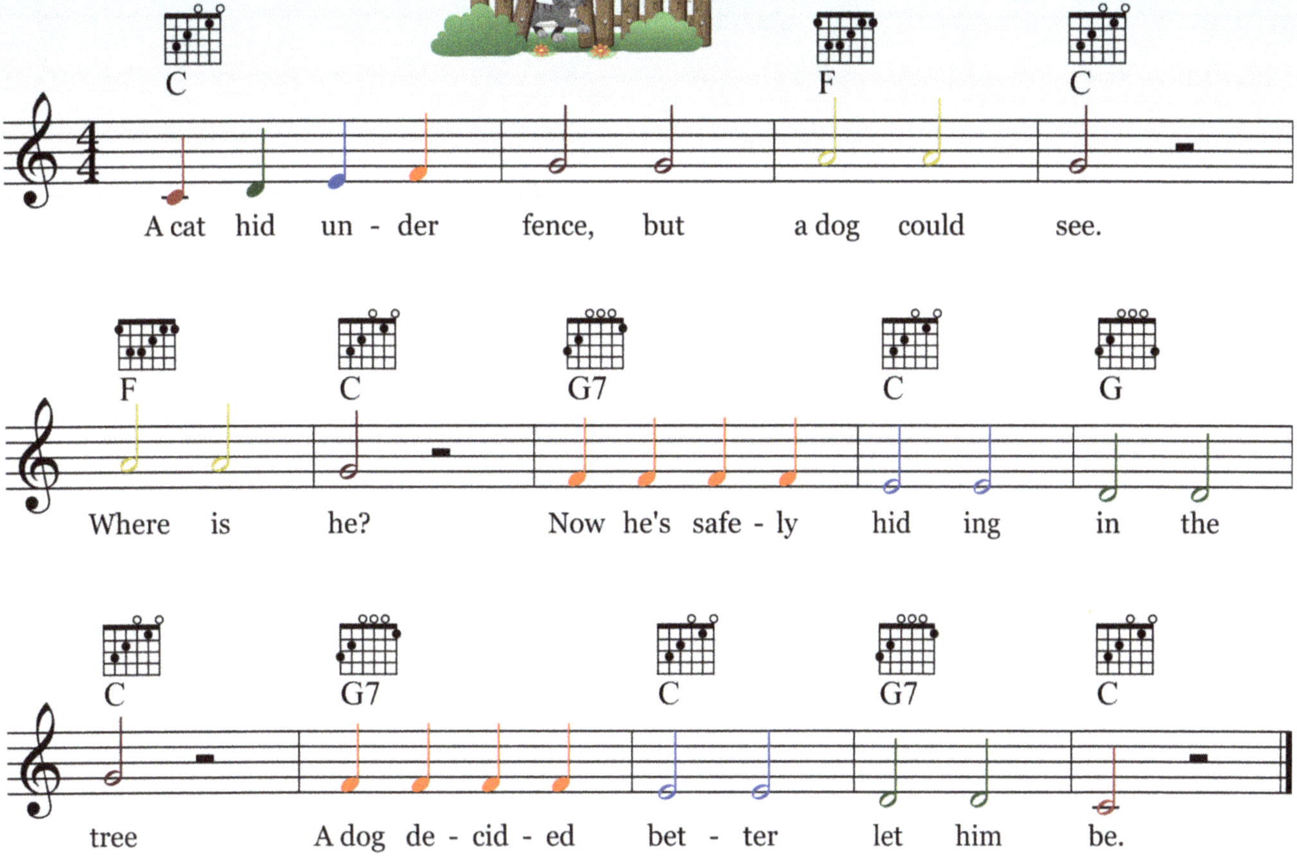

A Silly Dog Jumped Like a Frog
Page - 9

Little Vixen, Run!

Pages - 9, 11, 31

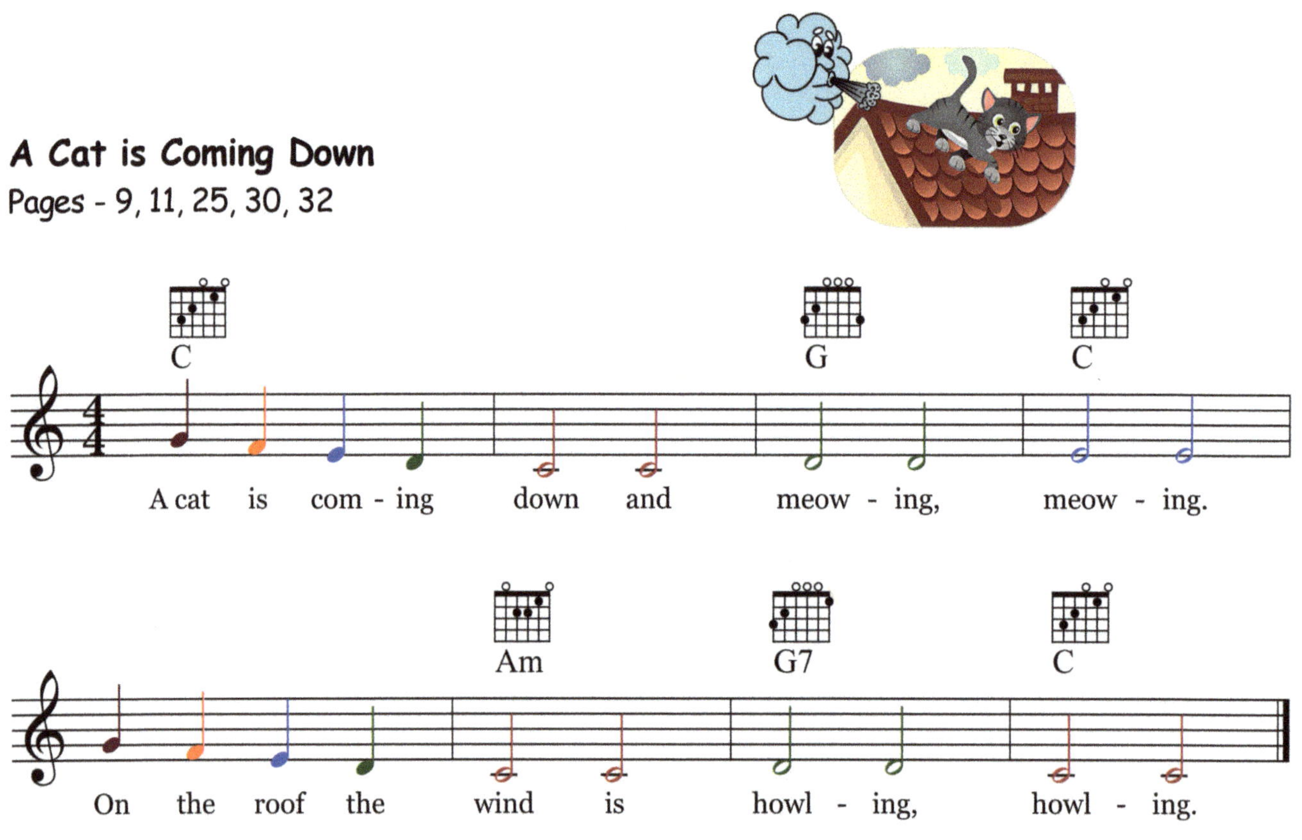

A Cat is Coming Down

Pages - 9, 11, 25, 30, 32

Rain is Falling, Work is Calling

Pages - 11, 30, 31

Mean Bagpiper

Page - 31

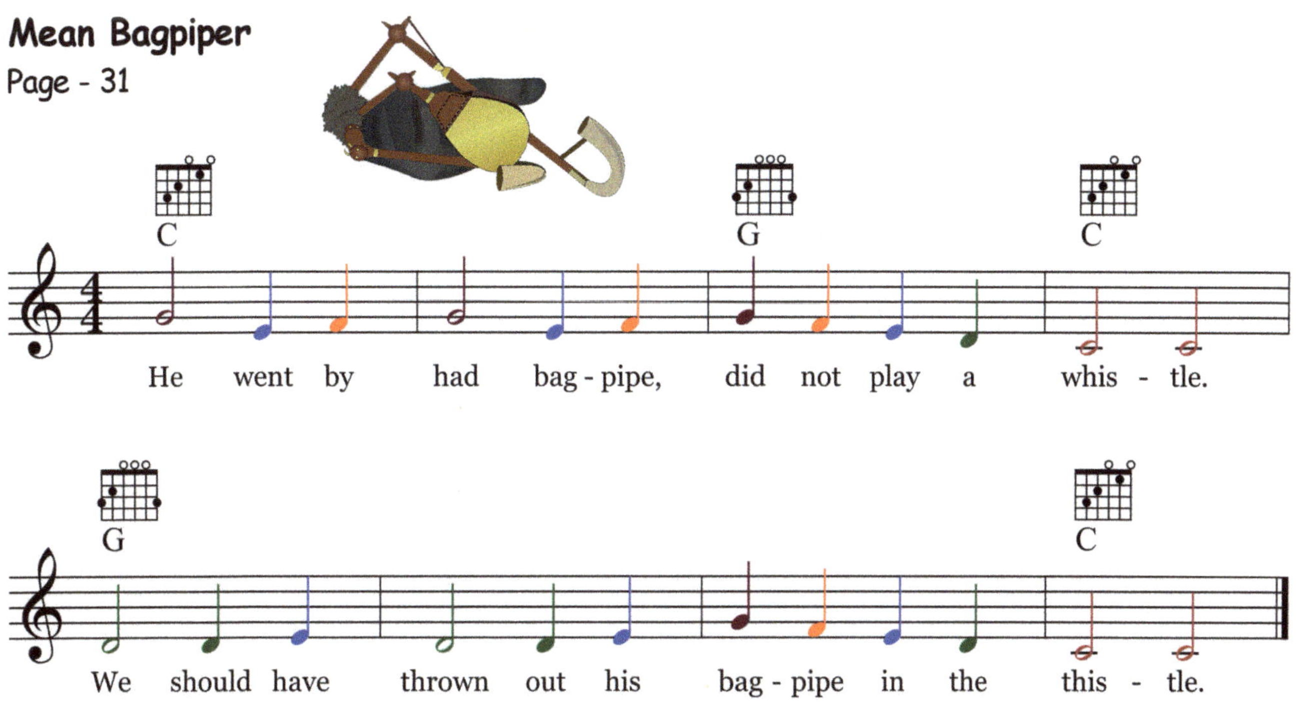

Hey-Ho, Little Sheep
Pages - 31, 45

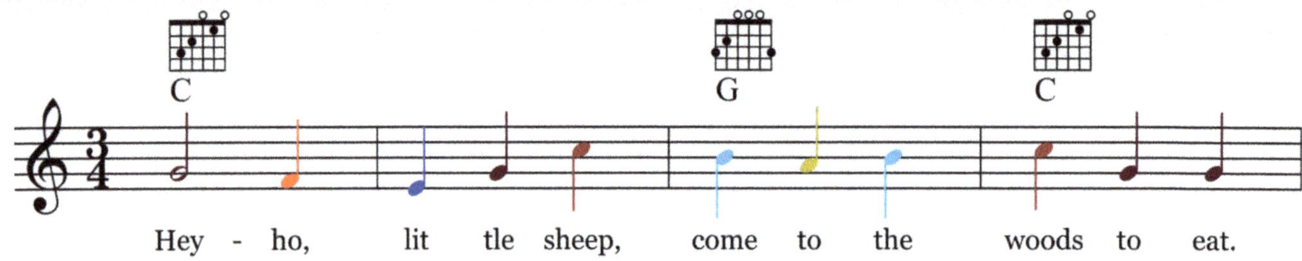

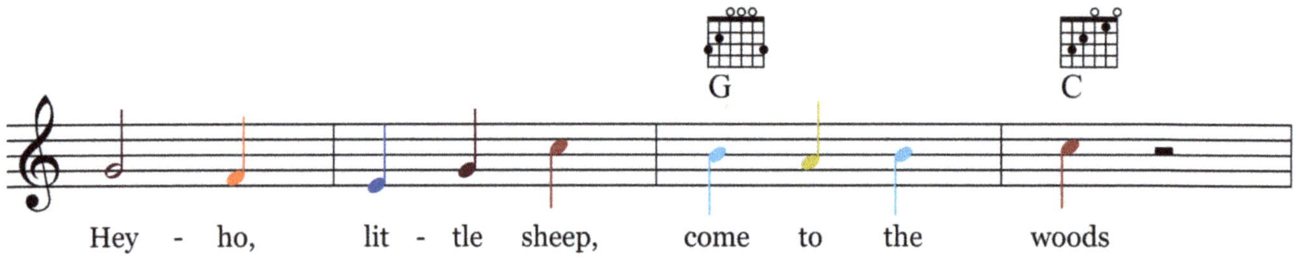

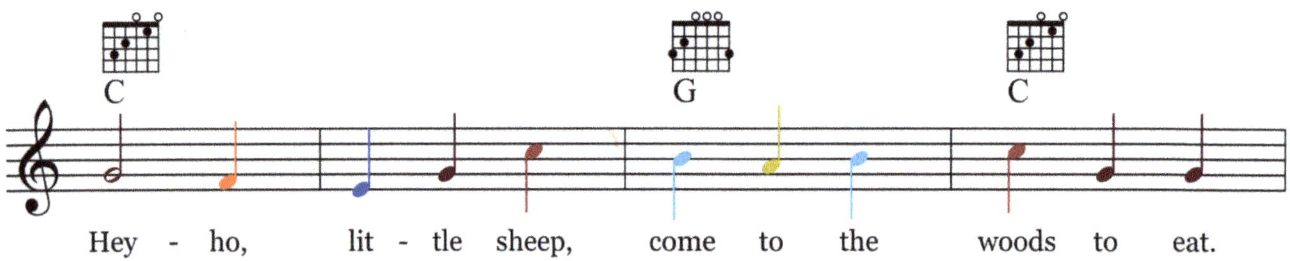

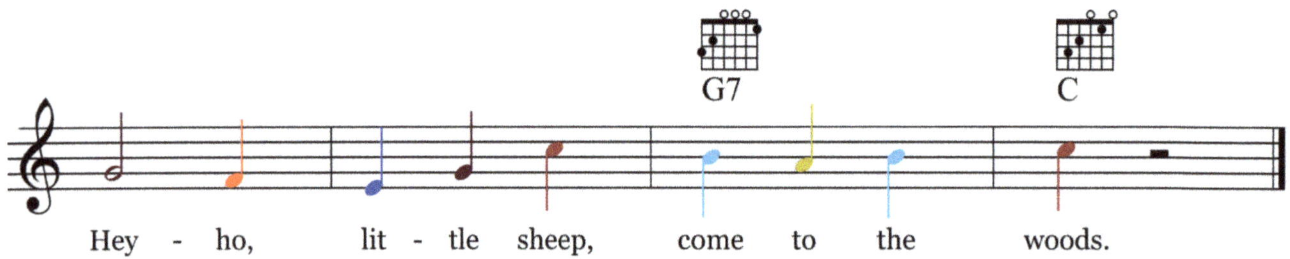

Our Fence Fell Down

Page - 32

C   G7

C

Run, Run, Run, Katy!

Page - 32

C   F   C

G   C

Am   G7   C

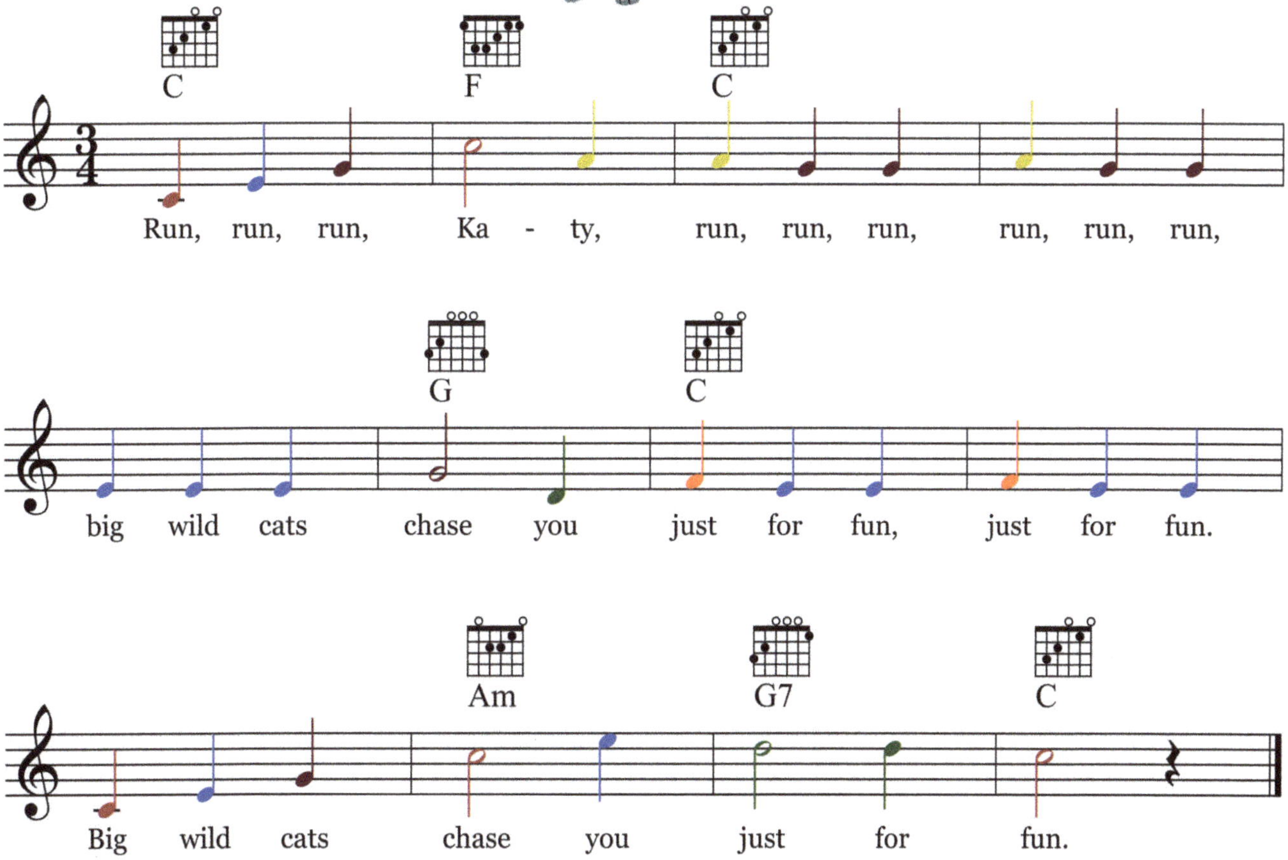

I Like Grass

Page - 32

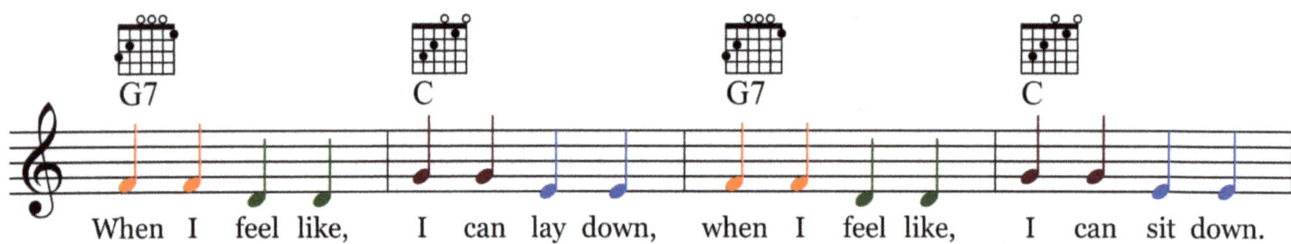

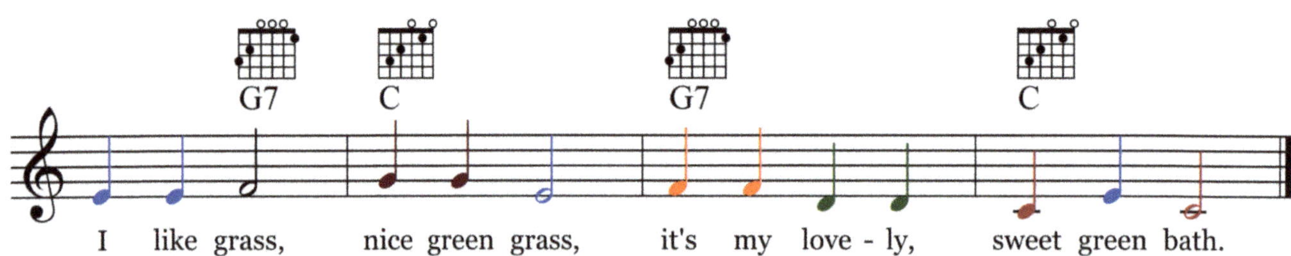

A Little Cuckoo Bird

Page - 41

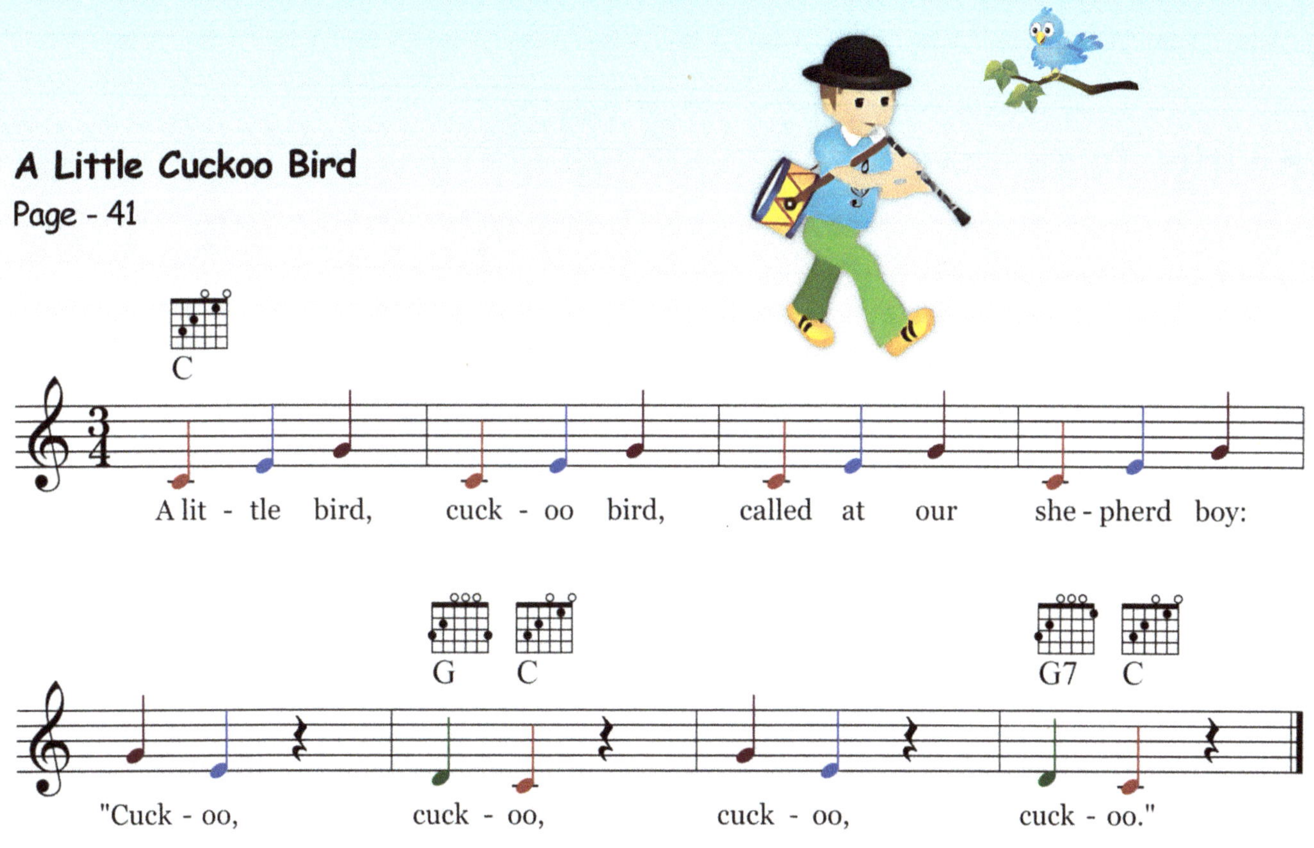

We Are Little Musicians

Page - 43

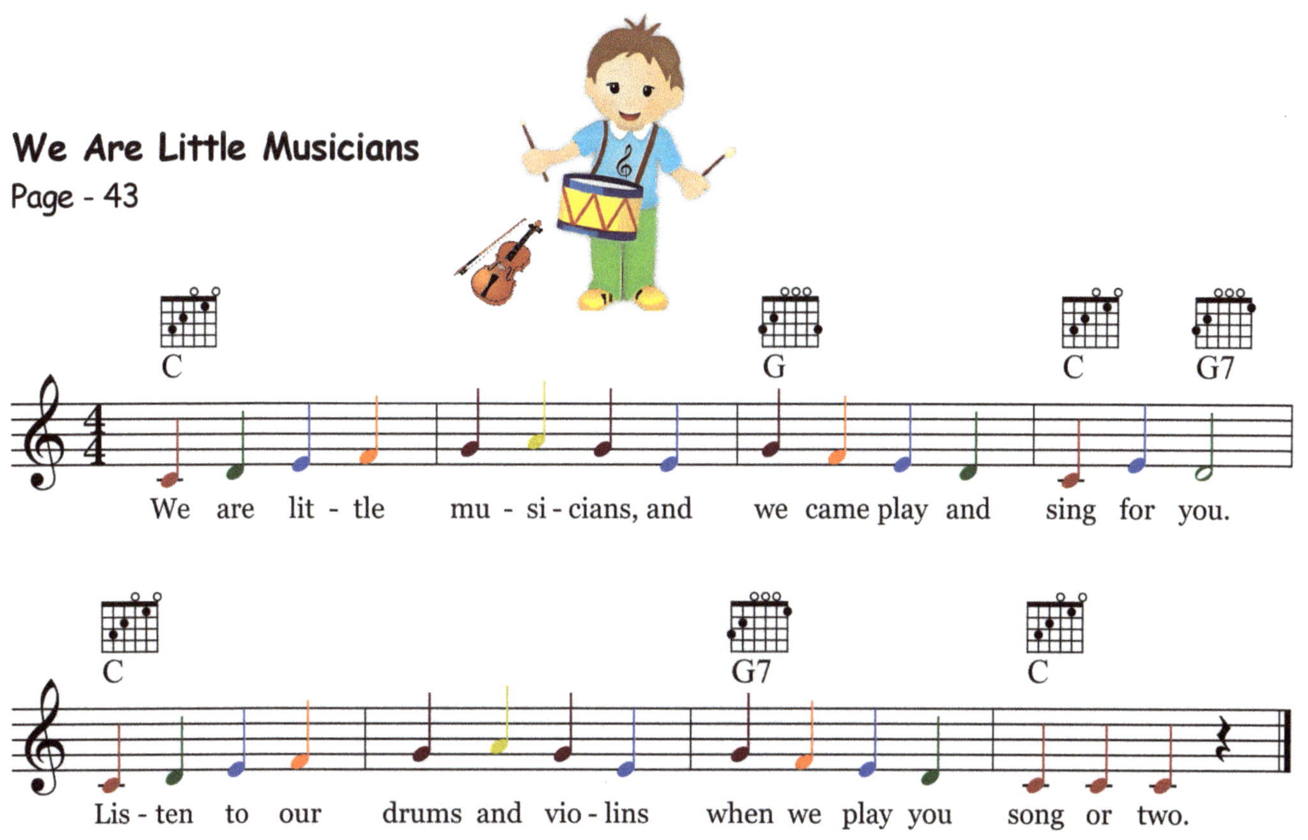

A Little Turtle Dove
Page - 45

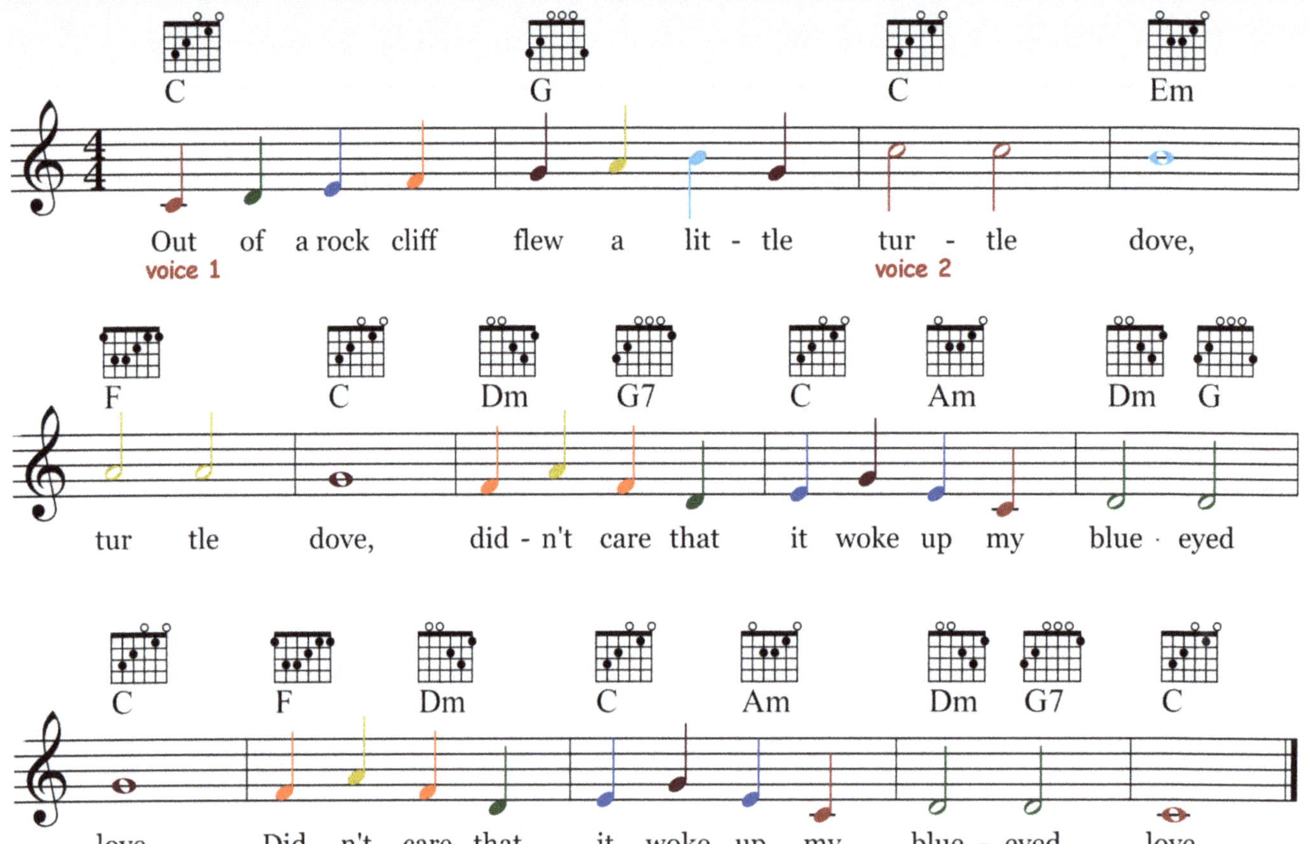

Little Turtle Dove is not only a beautiful song, but it is also a lovely **canon**.
Just try to sing in two groups, with the first starting and the second joining from the beginning of the song when the first group reaches the third measure. Clefi marked the voice entrances for you - **voice 1** and **voice 2**.

I Am a Musician

A little invitation to discover "Clefi's Musical Instruments!"

2. I am a musician...
   I play the violin. And how do you play it?
   |:Fiddle, tweedle dee, and needle, fiddle, tweedle, violin!:| cotton bin.

3. I am a musician...
   I will play my trumpet. And how do you play it?
   |:Tantara-ra (3 times), my trumpet!:| your crumpet.

4. I am a musician...
   I will play my guitar. And how do you play it?
   |:Pluck and strum, pluck, (3 times), guitar pluck!:| ducks do quack.

5. I am a musician...
   I play my piano. And how do you play it?
   |:Cling and clang, and clang and cling, and cling and clang, piano cling!:| cling let it ring.

Sleepy Adam
Page - 49 (the test song no. 2)

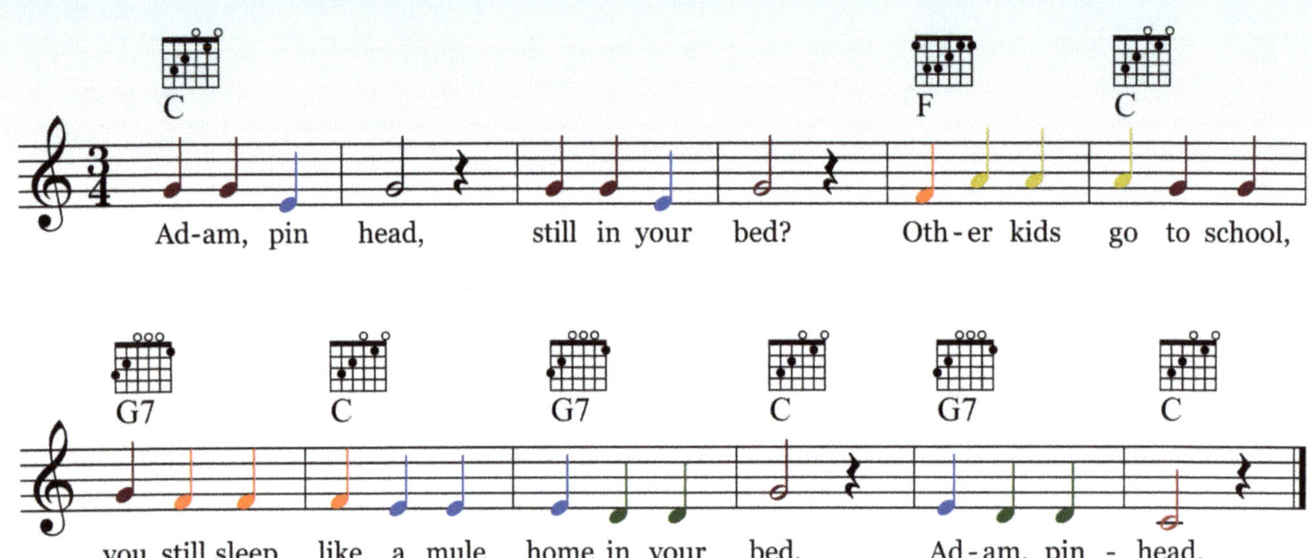

A little extra "High Five!" for your excellent work and "See you soon!" from Rex and Boo!

CERTIFICATE

OF COMPLETION

This certificate is presented to:

For successfully completing

Clefi's Little Notebook

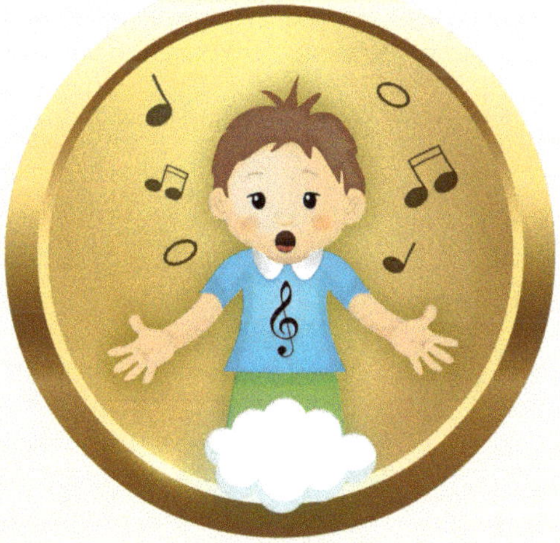

music education teacher

Clefi's Little American-British Music Dictionary

Music is a universal language; that is true. However, every nation uses its own beautiful tongue to describe and teach music. Clefi is originally Klíček, a little Czech boy who guides children through the fundamentals of music theory in Czech using the Czech language and music terminology. His American twin brother, Clefi, had to translate and adapt the text so English-speaking children could enjoy the journey. However, not all English-speaking musicians use the same music terms. Therefore, Clefi created this little American-British Music Dictionary of music terms used in this book to accommodate our British English-speaking music friends.

Note Values

Whole note	Semibreve
Half note	Minim
Quarter note	Crotchet
Eighth note	Quaver

Note Distances

Whole step	Tone
Half step	Semitone

Octaves

Fourth octave	One-line octave
Fifth octave	Two-line octave

Notes

C4-B4	c'-b' (one-line c-b)
C5	c'' (two-line c)

www.bumblebeenotes.com/clefis-musical-world

www.bumblebeenotes.com/music-publishing